A Leader's Guide to Knowledge Management

A Leader's Guide to Knowledge Management

Drawing on the Past to Enhance Future Performance

John P. Girard, Ph.D.
Minot State University

JoAnn L. Girard
Sagology

A Leader's Guide to Knowledge Management
Copyright © Business Expert Press, LLC, 2009.

First published in 2009 by
Business Expert Press, LLC
222 East 46th Street, New York, NY 10017
www.businessexpertpress.com

ISBN-13: 978-1-60649-018-1 (paperback)
ISBN-10: 1-60649-018-4 (paperback)

ISBN-13: 978-1-60649-019-8 (e-book)
ISBN-10: 1-60649-019-2 (e-book)

DOI 10.4128/9781606490198

A publication in the Business Expert Press Strategic Management collection

Collection ISSN: 2150-9611 (print)
Collection ISSN: 2150-9646 (electronic)

Cover design by Artistic Group—Monroe, NY
Interior design by Scribe, Inc.

First edition: May 2009

10 9 8 7 6 5 4 3 2 1

Printed in the United States of America.

Abstract

Today when most executives consider the intellectual capital of their organization, they focus on the present. They seek tools and techniques to exploit their organizational knowledge for some immediate gain. There is an emerging shift in thinking that will provide a lasting competitive advantage—the shift is from the present to the future. This book is unique in that it focuses on what executives should be doing now (or soon) to ensure the next generation of organizational leaders know what we knew. In other words, are we creating organizational memories today, which will be useful to the next generation of leaders? Will today's babyboomer based practices pass the test of time? Are our current processes the most relevant ones for the next generation of organizational leaders?

To answer these questions the book is divided into three parts. Part 1 is introductory in nature and provides a concise overview of knowledge management: its genesis, the theory of knowledge, and the types of knowledge that exist. Part 2 builds on this foundation and highlights some of the successes and failures during the past two decades as babyboomer executives struggled to develop effective ways of sharing what their organizations know. A review of projects suggests that many firstgeneration knowledge management projects were based on collecting and classifying information. Second-generation knowledge management projects shifted the focus to codifying tacit knowledge and combining explicit knowledge to create new knowledge.

Part 3 focuses on emerging ideas that show great potential. Today we are seeing some very promising results from third-generation knowledge management projects, which focus on connecting people and facilitating collaboration. Some pioneering organizations are now reaping the benefits of using social media tools such as wikis for collaboration and commercial social networking tools, for connecting people. These emerging tools and techniques provide flexible, agile, and intuitive solutions for connecting people with people and facilitating coordination, communication, and collaboration.

Keywords

knowledge management, enterprise dementia, sagology, Torii, future, leadership, technology, culture

Contents

Figures

Welcome

Welcome to *A Leader's Guide to Knowledge Management: Drawing on the Past to Enhance Future Performance*. We are delighted that you have decided to embark on this journey of discovery. We hope that you enjoy this book as much as we enjoyed writing it!

At a recent conference, the keynote speaker suggested that just about everything that needed to be known about *Knowledge Management* already existed. We think he was referring to the seminal works in the domain, such as Nonaka and Takeuchi's *The Knowledge-Creating Company* (1995), O'Dell and Grayson's *If Only We Knew What We Know* (1998), Davenport and Prusak's *Working Knowledge* (1998), and perhaps a few others. He suggested there was no need for any more books, but rather executives should start applying the ideas that already existed. Ironically, he was at the conference to promote his new book about managing knowledge!

We agree that ample resources exist for the executive who wishes to manage his or her organizational intellectual property. Perhaps we should qualify this statement. We know that proven tools and techniques exist to manage today's knowledge assets. But what about the future? Will today's babyboomer-based practices pass the test of time? Are our current processes the most relevant ones for the next generation of organizational leaders?

This book builds on the many great works in the knowledge management domain; however, it is unique in that we focus on what we should be doing now (or soon) to ensure the next generation of organizational leaders *knows what we knew*. In other words, are we creating organizational memories today that will be useful to the leaders who follow us?

We have worked diligently to provide a concise, no-nonsense view of knowledge management. Given that we believe that information overload is a challenge confronting many leaders today, we did not want to contribute to the bombardment. To that end, we have carefully selected the material we included to ensure it will be valuable for you. For those who desire more knowledge, we have included a comprehensive list of more than 100 references. We have also highlighted what we consider the *must-read* books in the domain. If we mention a book by title, that is our recommendation for you to add it to your reading list.

We would be remiss if we did not acknowledge that many people helped us with this book, some directly and others indirectly. Without people such as Nick Bontis, Carla O'Dell, Bob Buckman, Steve Denning, Dave Snowden, and many other authors, we would not have had a foundation from which to build—thanks for your hard work and inspiration. A special thanks goes to Sandy Lambert, who helped us develop the material for Chapter 7. Finally, we thank the team at Business Expert Press, especially David Parker and Mason Carpenter, for their advice and patience as we developed the manuscript.

—John and JoAnn

PART 1

Drawing on the Past

CHAPTER 1

Where Is the Knowledge?

Where is the wisdom we have lost in knowledge?
Where is the knowledge we have lost in information?

—T. S. Eliot, *The Rock* (1935)

The works of poet T. S. Eliot appear regularly in management books, even though he technically was not a management guru. So why is it that so many of us turn to a poet rather than an academic, corporate executive, or some other management pundit when we feel the need to explain how knowledge is lost in organizations? Surely, a poet from another century is not the leading authority on creating and exchanging enterprise knowledge.

T. S. Eliot's frequent quotation is likely because he so eloquently stated what many of us try to express when he penned the prose above. These two lines from the opening chorus of *The Rock* articulate the knowledge management dilemma. One would assume the aim is to gain, not lose, wisdom and knowledge as managers ascend the cognitive hierarchy. That said, it seems T. S. Eliot's questions are more valid today than when they were scribed so long ago (Girard, 2006).

We begin our exploration of knowledge with an examination of the building blocks. Just as a mason must have a sound understanding of his or her tools before building a magnificent structure, we must understand the bricks and mortar of our structure. The bricks of our craft are knowledge, and the glue that holds this together is knowledge management, akin to our mortar. The focus of the first part of this book is on how to build a solid foundation of knowledge on which we will build organizational memories.

Some people may argue that there is no need to learn this foundational material. We cannot imagine a mason constructing a cathedral without understanding the different types of bricks and mortar that are at his or her disposal. In the same way, the executive who is responsible for designing, implementing, and maintaining organizational memories must strive for an absolute comprehension of the knowledge necessary to manage this critical resource.

Much as it is very difficult to repair the foundation of a large building, it is very time-consuming and expensive to reengineer the knowledge architecture of a poorly designed organizational memory system. In the construction industry, there are strict building codes, often based on experience, to guide our actions. In the knowledge industry, the codes are far less well defined. An implicit aim of this book is to help steer you by providing some guiding principles. These principles are not as explicit as the building codes, but they may go some way in aiding your construction project.

So do we really need to discuss knowledge management and ideas such as dealing with organizational memory loss? We think the answer is yes, but you can be the judge. The following is a real-world example of why this is important; there are many others in the pages ahead.

During an interview on CBS News on September 11, 2006, New York Fire Department Deputy Fire Chief John Norman described the unfathomable loss of life of the Department's Special Operations Command five years earlier. On that tragic day, September 11th, 2001, Special Operations Command lost 95 men—totaling 1600 years of experience.

This is simply unimaginable when one considers this specialized unit pioneered techniques for urban rescue and terrorist attacks. Surely, it would be impossible to reconstitute the unique and vital knowledge of these brave men. Norman's team proved that they had plans in place to quickly rebuild their team and once again become the best in the world. Five years later, the knowledge loss of the team was virtually unnoticeable as the team responded to 50 calls. (Pitts, 2006)

This story is not meant to demean the heartbreaking loss of very brave men, but rather it is to commemorate the outstanding leadership, courage, and culture of a team that would not give up. Fortunately, most organizations do not have to suffer the tragic loss that Norman described, but perhaps we can learn from their tragedy. Virtually all organizations must deal with organizational memory loss to varying degrees. Could your organization rebuild from such devastation? What are you doing today to make sure the next generation of leader is as well prepared as Deputy Fire Chief John Norman?

So What Is the Problem?

To some degree, the problem is about Eliot's second line: *Where is the knowledge that we have lost in information?* Many managers seem to be swamped by the quantity of information in their organizations. A recent KPMG knowledge management study reported that two-thirds of the sample complained of information overload (Parlby, 2000). A second study determined that 38% of the surveyed managers waste a substantial amount of time locating information and that 43% of the managers delayed decisions because of too much information (Wilson, 2001). A Gartner Research report suggests that a major driver of this problem is distraction since many managers "dwell on information that is entertaining but not informative, or easily available but not of high quality" (Linden, 2001, p. 2). A June 2008 *Business Week* article suggested 28% of an average U.S. worker's day is wasted dealing with these distractions, perhaps reducing productivity by $650 billion (Jackson, 2008). A myriad of other studies report similar disturbing findings that appear to be information related (Bawden, 2001; Feldman, 2004; Speier, Valacich, & Vessey, 1999; Wilson, 2001).

From these studies, one may deduce that managers suffer from information bombardment and yet they seem to crave more information. This vicious cycle is caused because most of the material available to these managers is unstructured and not of much value. In other words, these managers are dealing with data or information instead of the sought after knowledge (Girard, 2006). Ironically, the more information many managers receive, the more they yearn for even more information, further compounding the crisis. However, what if that all changed and these overloaded managers abandoned their quest for information and began an expedition for that elusive entity titled knowledge?

Knowledge management is becoming the panacea of the 21st century or so many organizational gurus would have you believe. Quarterly journal articles add to the tomes on knowledge management; nonetheless, there appears to be absolute bewilderment over the meaning of the expression. Although knowledge management is often the subject of boardroom discussions, business and government leaders seldom understand the subject. Instinctively, they yearn for the ability to manage their enterprise knowledge, whatever that is, without truly appreciating the potential benefits or pitfalls of knowledge management (Girard, 2004b).

It has been said, "In an economy where the only certainty is uncertainty, the only sure source of lasting competitive advantage is knowledge" (Nonaka, 1991, p. 8). What a powerful idea, an idea that many of us embrace. But what does this mean? How can we apply this powerful idea in a business environment? Equally important, we would argue, are the factors that create this uncertainty such as globalization, deregulation, technology, terrorism, the economy, downsizing, and information overload. Of these reasons to consider a knowledge management initiative, the last two explain why knowledge management ought to be an immediate priority in order to achieve a sustainable organizational advantage for profit, not-for-profit, and government organizations.

The Future—Will It Be Better?

So if information tribulations exist today, what will the future hold? Not surprisingly, the amount of data and information available will increase in the future, but by how much? The number of books published annually has increased exponentially since the 16th century. At present, the prediction is that the number of books doubles every 33 years (Hanka & Fuka, 2000). A separate report corroborates this harsh reality by suggesting humankind produced more information in the last three decades than in the previous five millenniums (White & Dorman, 2000).

If one considers the total accumulated codified database of the world, which includes all books and all electronic files, the doubling occurs every 7 years (Bontis, 2001). Tragically, this total codified database includes a significant amount of unprocessed, unstructured, or duplicate data. This mountain of unprocessed data is becoming so large that it is smothering itself and preventing its metamorphosis to knowledge. Recent research suggests that it may be quicker for scientists to repeat experiments rather than search for previous results (White & Dorman, 2000). This attitude further acerbates the problem by the creation of more duplicate data. Clearly, current practices will not permit managers to cope with the predicted data explosion.

Downsizing is often an unfortunate partner in the information surplus challenge. A by-product of the reorganization/reengineering trends of the late 20th century is that most organizations—both profit and not-for-profit—now boast leaner structures. From a knowledge management perspective, this creates a number of new and unanticipated tribulations especially for managers. For example, according to the president of the Canadian Public Service, there was a 25% decrease in the number of executives in the 1992 to 2001 period (Serson, 2001). The economic crisis of 2009 may once again force organizational leaders to reconsider organizational structures. What will be the impact of this exercise?

Middle managers have an opportunity to fulfill an important information and knowledge filtering function (DeTienne & Jackson, 2001). Unfortunately, a consequence of the reduction or elimination of middle managers is the loss of this critical information filter. In the past, subordinate managers would filter messages before presenting them to executives. This sieving not only eliminated the quantity of worthless messages but it also provided an opportunity for middle managers to improve the value of the message. These middle managers would transform data to information or information to knowledge. The result was fewer but higher quality messages and therefore more valuable messages arriving on the senior executives' desks. This reduction in the number of messages decreases the time wasted, while the increase in quality diminishes the craving for more information. The synergy of this quantity–quality change provides management more time to concentrate on the important matters at hand.

A second challenge resulting from downsizing is a loss of tacit knowledge transfer previously associated with deliberate redundancy (Nonaka & Takeuchi, 1995). The structure of many organizations in the 1980s and before catered to understudies who would mature to become the next generation. Today this concept has all but evaporated, resulting in a disappointing consequence of knowledge loss. This shortfall necessitates the rediscovery of knowledge that was once resident within an enterprise—a task that often cascades to middle managers (Girard, 2005c).

The corollary to this is sometimes termed *organizational Alzheimer's*, which is "memory loss that occurs when key employees leave an organization, taking their [tacit] knowledge with them" (Galt, 2002). Research suggests that at least one-half of organizational knowledge is uncodified tacit knowledge (Horak, 2001). The departure of the human repository of this intellectual capital may take months or years of training and experience to replace—in the interim, the middle manager must somehow fill the knowledge void (Girard, 2005c).

Further exacerbating the effects of this tacit knowledge loss is the vast increase in retirements that some sections expect in the next decade. For example, according to a 2008 U.S. Government Accountability Office letter, 50% of the U.S. Department of Defense civilian workforce—a workforce of almost 700,000 people—will retire in the next few years (Farrell, 2008). In the 2008 report to Canada's prime minister, it was noted that 25% of Canadian Public Service executives are eligible to retire in the 5-year period starting in 2007. The report also highlighted that in 2012 nearly 50% of the Canadian Public Service executives who have been in an executive position since 2007 will be eligible for retirement (Lynch, 2008). These are but two examples of the impending knowledge crisis. We will consider others later in the book.

If organizations wish to seal this unnecessary memory leak and decrease the information overload of managers, they should invest in some sort of knowledge management. One solution is to provide a human understudy or apprentice, perhaps through the initiation of a mentoring program, much as was the norm yesteryear. Alternatively, they may opt for one of the knowledge management solutions introduced later in this book. The status quo of permitting corporate knowledge to flow freely from the organization and possibly directly to the competition is nonsensical (Girard, 2005c).

Enterprise Dementia

Although the term organizational Alzheimer's seems to be gaining in popularity, we believe that term is unnecessarily pessimistic. Clearly, the analogy accurately captures the memory loss and confusion typically associated with the terribly debilitating disease; however, most physicians agree that, at present, no cure exists for Alzheimer's. Conversely, the more general term of dementia, which includes similar ailments, is sometimes treatable especially when diagnosed early. This subtle difference is especially important as executives who accept the ideas within these pages will be well equipped to conquer the effects of the disease termed *Enterprise Dementia* (Girard, 2005c).

We would suggest that Enterprise Dementia comprises two closely related components: *Information Anxiety* and *Organizational Memory Loss*, both of which are very treatable. This relationship may go some way in explaining the unexpected and confusing results of a variety of recent research within the field of knowledge management. For example, two recent studies, completed by experts in the field, suggest that the implementation of a knowledge management program did not result in significantly less information overload (Parlby, 2000).

Surprising to some, one study found that 65% of respondents with a knowledge management program suffered from information overload while 69% of respondents without a knowledge management program suffered from information overload—hardly the vast improvement promised by so many gurus (Parlby, 2000). A Gartner Research study actually reported a 50% increase in information overload in knowledge management enabled organizations (Linden, Ball, Arevolo, & Haley, 2002). A more recent study of middle managers, which considered the type of managers, typical tasks, and knowledge transfer styles, determined that managers who employed the tenets of tacit knowledge management in decision making reported higher levels of anxiety than their counterparts who relied on explicit knowledge for their decisions (Girard, 2006). This was a real awakening for many consultants who suggested knowledge management as the great hope of the future.

What's Ahead

Perhaps the real question is, *Where is the knowledge we have lost in managers?* One wonders how organizations, which invested millions of dollars in programs to manage knowledge, are now discovering that their managers are less efficient than before the implementation. From an executive point of view, the question may be, *If knowledge is power, why am I always in the dark?* The follow-up question is almost certainly, *What can we do now to make sure my successors are not in the dark?*

The aim of this book is to consider the theory and practice of knowledge management with a view to answering the question, *Will the next generation of leaders know what you knew?* Unlike other books in the domain, this is not a book about the present, but rather it is a guide for the future. To be sure, we will spend some time reviewing what is working and not working today; however, the clear emphasis is building an organizational memory that will create value in the future. This memory, whatever that is, will be appreciated by the next generation of executives as they are challenged in ways we cannot even anticipate.

The text that follows examines a number of key concepts in the domain. We hope to present these ideas in a user-friendly style that combines academic theory, real-world best practices, and some personal observations. Each of the styles provides a different view of the same subject; however, together we hope this blend provides a précis of the current state of knowledge management as well as a very exciting glimpse of the future. Each chapter will end with two brief sections. First will be a *Remember* section, which will include a short review of one person discussed in the chapter. We hope that this section will be a good, albeit concise, way to remember the main theme of the chapter. Finally, we will include a very brief list of the main takeaways in the *Now You Know . . .* section.

Remember T. S. Eliot

Before moving on, it is worth reminding ourselves of what T. S. Eliot so eloquently penned: *Where is the wisdom we have lost in knowledge? Where is the knowledge we have lost in information?* These wise words remind us that many organizations are drowning in information while their executives are starving for knowledge. How does this apply to your organization? Are you reaping the benefits of your intellectual capital or is this potential benefit being lost due to enterprise dementia?

Now You Know . . .

- The amount of *information* produced in the last 30 years is greater than the amount produced in the previous 5,000 years.
- Downsizing contributes to a loss of *tacit knowledge.*

- **Enterprise Dementia** is a debilitating organizational ailment that comprises two closely related components: Information Anxiety and Organizational Memory Loss (Girard, 2005c).
- Knowledge management implementations do not ensure a reduction of information overload.
- Managers who rely on tacit knowledge for decision making sometimes report higher levels of information anxiety.

CHAPTER 2

Organize What?

Generally, management of the many is the same as management of the few.
It is a matter of organization.

—Sun Tzu (400–320 BC), *The Art of War*

Before considering the concept of *knowledge in action*, an understanding of some of the foundational theory is probably a good idea. In fact, it may be more than a good idea as we have been involved in too many discussions that seem to have been based on hype and emotions rather than the facts about the subject. We remember one particular development that illustrates this point. The story that follows is based on real events, but we changed it ever so slightly to *protect the innocent*. As we will discuss in a later chapter, a good story must be believable but not necessarily true.

Some time ago, one of us (John) was leading the knowledge management effort in a large organization. One day, an executive assistant asked to talk to John about knowledge management in general and more specifically about communities of practice. Later in the book there is more discussion on communities, but for now just think of a community of practice as a special type of group composed of passionate volunteers.

The executive assistant seemed almost desperate to learn about communities. John was a little surprised as the assistant had been quite resistant to John's near-evangelistic talks on the value of knowledge. Suddenly the executive assistant wanted to know everything about implementing communities of practice. To say John was suspicious would be an understatement. It was not that John did not want to help; of course he did. John was just wondering why he had transformed from a naysayer to the number one supporter of knowledge management in action.

In any case, John spent some time talking to him about communities. John gave him some in-house information on facilitating communities and recommended an upcoming training session being led by one of the real pioneers of communities, Etienne Wenger, the coauthor of *Cultivating*

Communities of Practice, an absolute must read for anyone interested in developing communities (Wenger, McDermott, & Snyder, 2002). A few weeks later, John met the executive assistant and was horrified, yet not really surprised, to hear that the community had failed. John said, "Do tell, what happened?" As it turned out, the executive assistant never did read the material that John gave him, nor did he attend the training sessions. He claimed not to have had the time!

Instead of learning from others who had experience in the domain, this young, motivated, and perhaps overeager manager launched a community that was destined for failure. It turns out he summoned a group of people from his organization, held a series of meetings in the boardroom, set some very difficult goals, missed most of the milestones, and then declared communities a waste of time. In fact, this group was not a community of practice; it was some sort of dysfunctional group. Calling it something that it was not—a community of practice—did not change the fact that it was simply a dysfunctional group.

We later discovered why this executive assistant became so interested in communities. It seems that his boss, a very senior executive, had just returned from a business trip. During a long flight, he read a short article about communities in action at the World Bank. Upon his return, he directed his assistant to set up a community so that their organization could reap the benefits of which he had read. Well, the rest is history. There are many morals of this story. We learned an important lesson: Excitement is not enough to guarantee success. A little bit of theory and background can go a long way in preparing for success!

The Theory of Knowledge

Admittedly, this section is introductory in nature and perhaps a little heavy on the academic theory of knowledge. For some, this section may feel like a return to school, but please bear with us. Think about the excited executive assistant and try not to repeat his mistakes! We truly believe that without a sound understanding of these fundamental concepts, it is difficult to appreciate fully the knowledge management arena.

Like the majority of academics and knowledge management authorities, we make a distinction between the three related but discrete terms of data, information, and knowledge. The three terms are hierarchical in nature with data being the foundation on which information builds to an apogee of knowledge. Sometimes we use the collective noun *knowledge* to group together the three blocks of the knowledge pyramid. For example, in *War and Anti-War*, the futurist authors Alvin and Heidi Toffler use the term knowledge as "defined broadly to include information, data, communication, and culture" (1993, p. 293). The outcome of such a broad definition is the belief that practices such as data processing, information management, and knowledge management are synonymous. Although that may suit their needs, we recommend avoiding such generalizations, at least until you fully appreciate the differences.

When we talk to groups about knowledge management, we often start with a short academic history of the discipline. We begin by discussing the groundbreaking work of one of the first knowledge management pioneers: Aristotle. Often people seem surprised to hear that the history of knowledge management began more than 2,000 years ago. It seems many people believe that knowledge management is new, something invented in business schools. Although the term knowledge management may be new, the concept of categorizing and defining the parts of knowledge is not new.

Sir Francis Bacon, attributed with saying "Knowledge is power," studied knowledge in the early 17th century and published his views in *The Advancement of Learning*. Despite this seminal work, interest in epistemology, or the study of knowledge, waned until post World War II. In the 1950s, there was tremendous progress in the cognitive sciences, which resulted in a resurgence of epistemological research. The point is that neither knowledge nor the study of knowledge is new (Grover & Davenport, 2001).

Today, several cognitive theories exist that take into account the pyramid of data, information, and knowledge. Some research suggests the hierarchy should extend beyond these three basic building blocks. For example, the U.S. Department of Defense (*FM 100-6: Information operations*, 1996) suggests the hierarchy should include a fourth component: Understanding. Systems theorist and professor of organizational change Russell Ackoff's (1994) hierarchy extended the Defense's pyramid to five by adding Wisdom. Other models, including Verna Allee's (1997) Knowledge Archetypes, enlarge the original three to seven by adding Meaning, Philosophy, Wisdom, and Union.

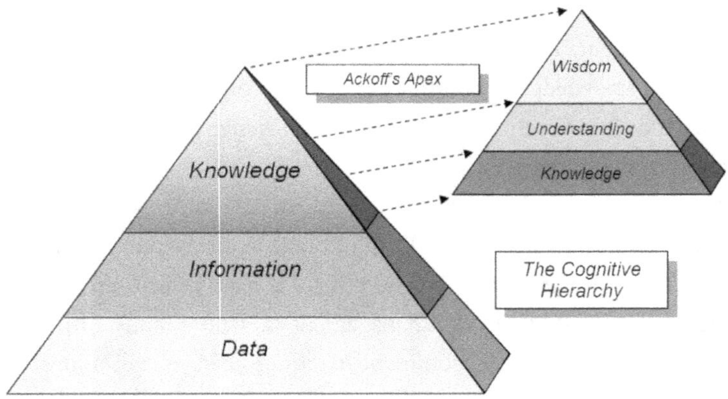

Figure 1. The Cognitive Hierarchy

Despite identical names for many of the components, there is no consensus on their exact meaning. As is often the case when academia and the business world merge, a variety of definitions exist for data, information, and knowledge. In *Working Knowledge*, two leading knowledge management experts, Thomas Davenport and Laurence Prusak (1998), suggest clear definitions for the three levels of the knowledge pyramid. Although not all pundits may accept these definitions, their work seems to provide a good launching point for our discussion.

Data–Information–Knowledge

The definition of data is almost certainly the least contentious, as it is relatively straightforward and intuitive. Davenport and Prusak define data "as a set of discrete, objective facts about events," and they suggest, "in an organizational context, data is most usefully described as structured records of transactions" (1998, p. 2). From a management perspective, two features are worthy of note. First, data is the lowest level in the value chain and by itself is not very beneficial. Arguably, too much data exists and until or unless managers transform this data into information, it is simply occupying valuable space. Second, data's symbolic nature permits ease of storage in and processing by computers. This characteristic drove the technical revolution of mechanical and then computer data processing, permitting machines to replace humans in the repetitive tasks of data entry (Girard, 2006).

Davenport and Prusak describe information as "a message, usually in the form of a document or an audible or visible communication" (1998, p. 3). Fundamental to their definition is the underlying assumption that a message must have a sender and a receiver. They suggest that "information is meant to change the way the receiver perceives something, to have an impact on his judgment and behavior" (1998, p. 3). This supports Peter F. Drucker's claim that "information is data endowed with relevance and purpose" (1988, p. 46). Combining these premises, one may deduce that the recipient, not the sender, is the real judge as to whether the packet received is data or information. In other words, even if a sender believes that information is being sent, the receiver may judge the package to be data if it does not have an impact on his or her perception, judgment, or behavior.

According to the authors of *Working Knowledge*, there are five major ways to transform data into information. First, one may put the data into *context* by communicating the reason for gathering the data. Second, one may *categorize* the data by describing the breakdown or the essential components of the data. Third, one may mathematically or statistically *calculate* the data. Fourth, one may *correct* errors in previously reported data. Finally, one may *condense* the data by providing a summary instead of the entire collection of data (Davenport & Prusak, 1998).

In reviewing the five "C's" of transforming data to information, we believe that technology may only assist in some forms of the transformation. For example, computers are very useful for calculating data; however, computers tend to be less able to assist in the contextual transformation. From this deduction, we offer that an increase in an organization's information technology resources will not necessarily improve the state of knowledge within the organization (Girard, 2006).

Authors Joseph and Jimmie Boyett suggest, "Knowledge is easy to talk about but hard to define" (2001, p. 104). Virtually all scholars agree that knowledge is above data and information in the value chain, but unfortunately the common ground ceases at this point. Beyond the basic recognition of an ordinal relationship, few academics or business leaders agree on the exact meaning of knowledge, despite more than 2,000 years of epistemology. The lack of a clear definition adds to the mystery of knowledge and enhances knowledge management's research appeal.

In *Working Knowledge*, the authors offer a definition that illustrates the value of knowledge and highlights the difficulty in managing knowledge. Despite the variety of definitions that exist, their definition is a great description of a rather complicated concept and a very good foundation to study knowledge management within organizations. Finally, this definition incorporates the spirit of the higher levels of the pyramid put forward in other models. Davenport and Prusak eloquently penned,

> Knowledge is a fluid mix of framed experience, values, contextual information, expert insight that provides a framework for evaluating and incorporating new experiences and information. It originates and is applied in the minds of knowers. In organizations, it often becomes embedded not only in documents or repositories but also in organizational routines, processes, practices, and norms. (Davenport & Prusak, 1998, p. 5)

Just as information is data that has a meaning or purpose, information may metamorphose into knowledge through a series of activities that increase its value. Returning to *Working Knowledge*, we see that four such activities transform information into the knowledge. First, one may *compare* information with previous information, primarily to determine what has changed in a particular situation. Second, one may determine the *consequences* or repercussions of this information on decisions. Third, one may consider how this information *connects* or correlates to other information. Finally, through *conversation* one may conclude what people think about the information (Davenport & Prusak, 1998).

A brief examination of these knowledge-enabling activities concludes that current computers are not particularly well suited for the transformation mission. These are tasks normally completed among people or inside an individual's mind. That is not to say that computers may not store the processed knowledge, much as books may store knowledge; however, computers rarely are able to execute the task of transforming information to knowledge. The vital inference is that knowledge management, unlike information management, will not generally be a technological solution; more often than not, knowledge management will comprise both human and technological components

(Girard, 2006). In fact, it is our belief that knowledge management is a human endeavor and cannot exist without humans.

Is There Really a Difference?

We are often asked if there really is a difference between these three entities. The question usually goes something like this: *OK, I agree that from an academic point of view there may be a difference, but is there really a difference from a practical point of view?* This is a great question and one that is definitely worthy of an answer. However, before answering the question directly we would like to describe the difference by using a piece of contemporary American art.

The October 27, 1917, cover of the *Saturday Evening Post* featured a beautiful painting by Norman Rockwell titled *Knowledge Is Power*.[1] The painting is of a room in which two people are standing; one is a 30-something-year-old man and the other is a young boy, perhaps 10 years old. The gentleman is properly dressed for the era, wearing a brown suit and carrying a trilby in one gloved hand. In his other hand is a small package beautifully wrapped and adorned with a red bow. Behind a large mahogany desk, a solemn-looking women is seated. On the desk, there are a few leather-bound books and a clock. The large hand of the clock points to the "8" and short hand points between the "4" and the "5." On a blackboard, the boy is writing the line "knowledge is power" repeatedly. Although he is facing the board, he is peering over his shoulder at the interaction between the two adults; a Cheshire cat smile adorns his youthful face. Few other details are visible in the painting.

John uses this painting in his graduate management classes. He starts by simply asking, "What time is it?" Most students quickly respond by saying 4:40 or perhaps 20 to five. In short, most students agree that by examining the clock we know the approximate time. John suggests to them that this is data—a simple fact. This often leads to interesting discussion about the reliability of the "fact" as invariably a few students will suggest that the clock could be broken or the time deliberately changed. This is an important idea to consider because if you believe that data may be

---

1. Given that a picture is worth a thousand words, you may wish to view the art at http://tinyurl.com/yx4syz

transformed through information to knowledge, then the accuracy of the data is vital. At the end of the discussion, most students agree that the time is 4:40 or perhaps 20 to five—a simple fact.

Next, John asks the question, "Where are these people?" Again, there is quickly consensus—they are in a classroom. "But how do you know?" he asks. In rapid succession students point out the features that helped form their decision: the blackboard, the desk, the teacher (woman), the books, the student (boy), chalk, and the list goes on. John suggests that each of these individual items may be data and alone insufficient to leap to the conclusion that this is a classroom. Surely not every room with a desk or room with a book is a classroom. They agree. In fact, he offers, they are putting data in context much as Davenport and Prusak described in *Working Knowledge*. The students agree that they have created information by putting data into context.

The final question is, "Why is the boy smiling?" Very quickly, it becomes apparent that consensus will elude the class. One student suggests, "He has just finished his 500th line and he is free!" Another suggests that "the man is his father who is late to pick him up," and next comes "the man is the teacher's boyfriend and the boy has caught the two together . . . knowledge is power!" Of course, all of these explanations make perfect sense and we may never know the real answer. When John proposes they have created knowledge, he is usually confronted with a sea of stares. In the ensuing discussion the students try to determine how there can be different but reasonable explanations of this new knowledge.

The class returns to our definition of knowledge, which is "Knowledge is a fluid mix of framed experience, values, contextual information, expert insight that provides a framework for evaluating and incorporating new experiences and information" (Davenport & Prusak, 1998, p. 5). What they have learned is that each of us views the information presented through a lens of experience. John suggests that the student who stated, "He has just finished his 500th line and he is free!" may have had a few *experiences* in detention. Likewise, the student who volunteered, "The man is the teacher's boyfriend and the boy has caught the two together . . . knowledge is power!" may have had the *experience* of being caught! This often-humorous exercise reminds us that data and information are mechanical in nature, and therefore it is relatively easy to achieve consensus. Quite to the contrary, knowledge is much more elusive and often our analysis of information will lead to different knowledge.

What Types of Knowledge Exist?

To return to the question is there a difference between data, information, and knowledge, we would argue that there is a significant difference—and the difference matters in organizations. So let us continue our exploration by examining knowledge itself. Is all knowledge the same? The answer to the question becomes very important as we consider the idea of managing knowledge. If all knowledge is the same, then presumably we will be able to design and build a structure, a process, or a technique that we may use to capture this knowledge for future use. If, on the other hand, there is more than one type of knowledge, then we may have to consider a multifaceted approach to packaging our knowledge.

Until relatively recently, most Westerners viewed the application of knowledge as a rigid and formal process. Through the application of practices and procedures, managers would apply knowledge to attain some measurable improvement in performance, typically something related to a better bottom line. In 1995, the award-winning book *The Knowledge-Creating Company: How Japanese Companies Create Dynamics of Innovation* began a knowledge revolution (Nonaka & Takeuchi, 1995). The spark for this revolution was the declaration that two distinct types of knowledge existed: tacit and explicit. Authors Ikujiro Nonaka and Hirotaka Takeuchi argued convincingly that the Japanese understanding and application of tacit knowledge provided a clear competitive advantage over the Western approach of explicit knowledge.

Nonaka and Takeuchi did not suggest that they invented the concept of tacit knowledge, but rather they chronicled the successes of Japanese executives in mastering the concepts. Aristotle was probably the first to make this distinction, though most forgot his revelation until Michael Polanyi, a chemist and philosopher, described the theory of tacit knowledge in his book *Personal Knowledge* published in 1958 (Polanyi, 1958). Even Polanyi's writings did not attract much attention until Nonaka reinvigorated interest over three decades later in a research paper titled "The Knowledge-Creating Company" (Nonaka, 1991)—the prequel to Nonaka and Takeuchi's seminal work of the same name.

Nonaka suggests explicit knowledge is "formal and specific . . . [and] can be easily communicated and shared" (Nonaka, 1991), while he and Takeuchi describe tacit knowledge as

> highly personal and hard to formalize, making it difficult to communicate and to share with others. Subjective insights, intuitions and hunches all fall into this category of knowledge. Furthermore, tacit knowledge is deeply rooted in an individual's action and experience, as well as in the ideals, values, or emotions he or she embraces. (Nonaka & Takeuchi, 1995, p. 8)

According to Nonaka and Takeuchi, one may segment tacit knowledge into two dimensions: technical and cognitive. They use a master artisan's gaining knowledge through experience to illustrate the technical dimension. Often these masters are unaware of the scientific or technical principles behind their work and yet they are able to create masterpieces. The cognitive dimension is based on individual's beliefs of what is today and what ought to exist in the future. Clearly, both tacit dimensions are very difficult to document or record in a computer. Conversely, explicit knowledge, which is based largely on known practices, procedures, and processes, is relatively easy to document.

Occasionally, when we talk about tacit knowledge, we see a series of blank stares, as if somehow the people just do not get it. We have tried a variety of ways to get our point across; however, none is as successful as describing one of our favorite television commercials. Great commercials are magic at quickly and vividly describing complex ideas in a short period and this example is one the best. The advertisement is for Bright-Stor storage software from Computer Associates and it goes something like this:

> The scene begins with an executive walking down a corridor flanked by two managers. The executive says, "So Dan, do we have everything we need for this meeting?" To which Dan says, while pointing to his temple, "It's all right here, sir." Dan turns to his fellow

manager and smiles like a Cheshire cat. As he rounds a corner, Dan, who is still smiling at his coworker, walks straight into an open filing cabinet drawer and falls to the floor. The executive and Dan's friend pause and look at Dan, who is out cold on the floor surrounded by files. The next scene sees the executive enter a full boardroom and sit at the head of the table. It is clear that this is an important meeting. Seconds later Dan's friend appears, leans over the executive, and says, "Don't worry, sir, he told me everything." At that exact moment, Dan's friend loses his balance and hits his head on the board table—he too is out cold. At this point a voice over says, "Is your data backup as secure as ours is?"

This humorous commercial is a very good reminder that most organizational knowledge is in the tacit form. Some people refer to this knowledge as the knowledge that goes home at night. No one knows for sure how much organizational knowledge is in this form—and to some degree it really does not matter whether it is 10% or 90% as the real question is, can you afford to lose this knowledge? Carla O'Dell, president of the APQC, uses an iceberg analogy to illustrate the point (O'Dell, 2002). She suggests that tacit knowledge is the knowledge below the waterline of the iceberg and explicit knowledge is the small portion above the water. As the captain of the Titanic learned, most of an iceberg is below the waterline.

The distinction between the two types of knowledge is a major reason why knowledge management is an exciting research area today. Without a clear understanding of this notion, Western knowledge management practices would have been unable to flourish. Until the 1990s, the focus of most Western knowledge management projects was the codification of explicit knowledge. In other words, they focused on documenting the formal and specific knowledge created by one person or organization to permit retrieval and utilization of this knowledge by others.

The Spiral of Knowledge

Central to Nonaka's thesis is the concept that new knowledge always begins with an individual—an idea that causes many information technology proponents to cringe. This notion is crucial to understanding

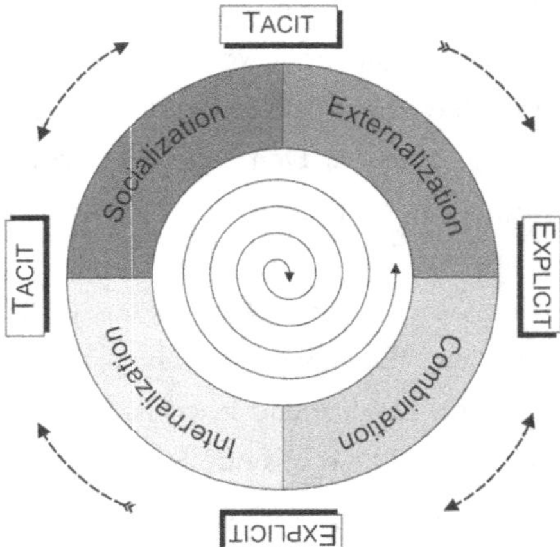

Figure 2. The Spiral of Knowledge (adapted from Nonaka &
Takeuchi, 1995)

knowledge and its relationship to management and therefore worthy of a brief review. Knowledge creation may take one of four forms: from tacit to tacit; from explicit to explicit; from tacit to explicit; or from explicit to tacit. A brief description of each of these concepts is below; we will explore some real-world applications of these concepts later in the book.

Nonaka and Takeuchi (1995) describe the transfer of tacit to tacit knowledge as socialization. Through social interaction, people may gain highly personal and difficult-to-formalize knowledge. One of the best examples is the apprentice shadowing the master artisan. Almost through osmosis, the young journeyperson learns the craft of the master. He or she will probably not understand the scientific principles underlying the master's skill but through socialization, the student slowly gains the knowledge required to replicate the teacher. At this point, the student crosses the threshold and becomes a master in his or her own right. Occasionally, the apprentice will surpass the master thus creating new tacit knowledge for the next generation of students.

The most common Western method of knowledge transfer is explicit to explicit or *combination* (Nonaka & Takeuchi, 1995). Through the process of codification, one person may document specific knowledge into some form of repository so that many others may access knowledge. An organization developing and formalizing best practices is a classic example of transferring explicit knowledge. Equally common is the creation of new knowledge by combining previously documented explicit knowledge.

The third concept of knowledge transfer or creation is foreign to Western thinkers. In this case, people strive to create or transfer tacit knowledge to the explicit form through *externalization* (Nonaka & Takeuchi, 1995). Using a previous example, one would wish to articulate or externalize the highly personal knowledge of the master artisan into an explicit form that is easier to formalize or document. For example, if one were able to shadow the artisan and deduce the application of scientific principles, then one could create new explicit knowledge.

The final classification, *internalization*, is the reverse of the previous notion, externalization (Nonaka & Takeuchi, 1995). The premise is knowledge creation through an amalgamation of codified explicit knowledge and fuzzy tacit knowledge. Consider the master artisan who educates himself in the sciences and through this education and his intuition is able to develop a better way to produce his craft.

The four concepts of knowledge creation need not operate in isolation. In fact, organizations or managers who believe in Nonaka's tenets would wish to maximize the use of each method of exchanging and transferring knowledge. Imagine the middle manager who patiently observes executives at work. Through socialization, she slowly learns the inner working of the boardroom. In an effort to formalize her knowledge, she articulates or externalizes the executives' ideas into a series of procedures based on economics principles. By combining the codified procedures of several managers, she develops and documents new concepts. Finally, she presents these new concepts to a number of managers, perhaps at a conference, and they internalize the ideas and create even better ways of affecting their technique and thereby creating a competitive advantage. At this point, the process may recommence.

Remember Dan

Our story about Dan exemplifies the need to consider your organization's tacit knowledge. Remember that many organizations assume, or perhaps hope, that the tacit knowledge that goes home at night will be back the next morning. What would be the implications in your organization? Could you survive and compete with a loss of tacit knowledge? Of course, we do not want or need to codify all of tacit knowledge, but perhaps there are some particular knowledge nuggets that deserve special attention. In any case, do not fall victim the way that Dan's boss did, so plan ahead.

Now You Know . . .

- The study of knowledge management is not new; in fact, it has been studied for at least 2,000 years.
- The cognitive hierarchy includes data, information, and knowledge; some authorities expand the original three to include understanding and wisdom.
- **Data** is a set of discrete, objective facts about events; in an organizational context, data is most usefully described as structured records of transactions (Davenport & Prusak, 1998, p. 2).
- **Information** is a message, usually in the form of a document or an audible or visible communication (Davenport & Prusak, 1998, p. 3). Fundamental to this definition is the underlying assumption that a message must have a sender and a receiver. Information is meant to change the way the receiver perceives something, to have an impact on his judgment and behavior (Davenport & Prusak, 1998, p. 3). Peter F. Drucker suggested, "Information is data endowed with relevance and purpose" (1988, p. 46).
- **Knowledge** is a fluid mix of framed experience, values, contextual information, and expert insight that provides a framework for evaluating and incorporating new experiences and information. It originates and is applied in the minds of knowers. In organizations, it often becomes embedded not only in documents or repositories but also in organizational routines, processes, practices, and norms (Davenport & Prusak, 1998, p. 5).
- **Tacit Knowledge** is highly personal and hard to formalize, making it difficult to communicate and to share with others. Subjective insights, intuitions, and hunches all fall into this category of knowledge. Furthermore, tacit knowledge is deeply rooted in an individual's action and experience, as well as in the ideals, values, or emotions he or she embraces (Nonaka & Takeuchi, 1995).

- **Explicit Knowledge** is "formal and specific . . . [and] can be easily communicated and shared" (Nonaka, 1991).
- **Socialization** is the transfer of tacit to tacit knowledge (Nonaka & Takeuchi, 1995). Through social interaction, people may gain highly personal and difficult-to-formalize knowledge. One of the best examples is the apprentice shadowing the master artisan. Almost through osmosis, the young journeyperson learns the craft of the master. He or she will probably not understand the scientific principles underlying the master's skill, but through socialization, the student slowly gains the knowledge required to replicate the teacher.
- **Externalization** is the transfer of tacit knowledge to the explicit form (Nonaka & Takeuchi, 1995). For example, one may wish to articulate or externalize the highly personal knowledge of a master artisan into an explicit form that is easier to formalize or document.
- **Combination** is the transfer of explicit to explicit knowledge (Nonaka & Takeuchi, 1995). Through the process of codification, one person may document specific knowledge into some form of repository so that many others may access knowledge. An organization developing and formalizing best practices is a classic example of transferring explicit knowledge. Equally common is the creation of new knowledge by combining previously documented explicit knowledge.
- **Internalization** is the transfer of explicit knowledge to the tacit form (Nonaka & Takeuchi, 1995). The premise is knowledge creation through an amalgamation of codified explicit knowledge and fuzzy tacit knowledge. Consider the master artisan who educates himself in the sciences and through this education and his intuition is able to develop a better way to produce his craft.

CHAPTER 3

What Types of Knowledge Exist?

Scientia protenia est (Latin maxim, "For also knowledge itself is power.")

—Sir Francis Bacon, *Meditationes Sacrae* (1597)

In this chapter, we introduce a new model of knowledge management enablers that we designed to help leaders conquer the knowledge challenges of today. The review begins with an overview of the knowledge challenges facing organizations. Next, a review of a number of knowledge management models concludes that five enablers are the most important. These five enablers are molded together to form a new exemplar based on the Japanese structure of the Torii. The results of a quantitative research project validate the Torii's components of Technology, Leadership, Culture, Process, and Measurement.

Practitioners and academics alike suggest that knowledge management might be the solution to many organizational challenges. Frequent journal articles add to the body of knowledge in the domain of knowledge management and yet we seem no closer to the Holy Grail. In the last decade, management gurus have offered a variety of reasons why leaders should consider knowledge management as a way ahead. Some of the more popular suggestions include deregulation, globalization, technology, terrorism, downsizing, and information overload. Though each of these notions bears merit, the last two demand the attention of organizational leaders as they seem to be widespread in so many organizations—public, private, not-for-profit.

This chapter is the culmination of a research project that began several years ago. Through formal presentations to various groups, the ideas of the project have been refined. The aim of this chapter is to provide executives a model that may be useful in combating these destructive forces, which unfortunately are commonplace in our organizations of today. The review begins with an overview of several contemporary knowledge management models from which five enablers emerge as the most important for organizations that wish to succeed in the future. These five components are blended to create a new archetype. The model was included in a recent survey instrument with a view to conducting exploratory research into the viability of the model. Although space constraints preclude a detailed analysis of the quantitative results, a brief summary of the study and the major findings are included.

What Are the Knowledge Management Enablers?

In the previous chapter, we defined the component parts and concepts of knowledge management. Using an analogy of the knowledge pyramid, the concentration, thus far, has been on the data foundation or facts about knowledge management. This chapter builds on this foundation by adding relevance or purpose: in other words, layer two of the pyramid, analogous to information.

The review of knowledge management enablers commences by considering the findings published in *If Only We Knew What We Know* (O'Dell, Grayson, & Essaides, 1998). This work is a first-class project that dedicates a substantial effort to describing the results of their research to what they term *the enablers of transfer*. In developing their thesis, O'Dell and Grayson had access to a number of knowledge management research projects completed by the APQC. Few other researchers have utilized such a comprehensive database to develop their theories.

O'Dell and Grayson contend that "Infrastructure, culture, technology and measurement are all necessary enablers [of knowledge management]; none alone is sufficient. Rather, they must all work in concert to achieve sustainable success" (O'Dell et al., 1998, p. 71). The premise that a number of interrelated and interdependent elements comprise the knowledge management model is grounded in system theory and supported by other recent research (Calabrese, 2000; Mohamed, Stankosky, & Murray, 2004; Weber, Wunram, Kemp, Pudlatz, & Bredehorst, 2002). Though we agree with O'Dell and Grayson's premise, it is important to underscore Leadership as an enabler as suggested by many others (Mohamed et al., 2004; Weber et al., 2002). O'Dell and Grayson acknowledge the importance of leadership as an enabler; however, they opted to have leadership subsumed in each category rather than as a stand-alone subject area. Though there is considerable merit in their assumption, leadership is worthy of its own discussion.

Current Knowledge Management Enabler Models

At present, a number of models exist that attempt to describe the enablers of knowledge management. The scope of this chapter prohibits a comprehensive review of the entire spectrum of current models, but nor is that necessary. Rather, it is important to acknowledge that a variety of models exists and to recognize that consensus has not been achieved. Despite the lack of harmony, a review of contemporary thinking is worthwhile as it provides a primer of best practices.

Three of the most well-known models are worth a brief review. First is *Knowledge Management: The Architecture of Enterprise Engineering*; next is the European network for knowledge management; and finally, the U.S. Department of Navy's *Balanced Knowledge Management* model. These three models provide a comprehensive overview of current thinking, both from an academic and from a practitioner's view. Equally, these exemplars provide a brilliant balance between profit and not-for-profit organizations, as well as U.S. and European ideas. In the following section, each of these models is compared and contrasted with O'Dell and Grayson's framework.

Developed by Dr. Stankosky and his team at George Washington University in 1999, *Knowledge Management: The Architecture of Enterprise Engineering* is colloquially termed the *Pillars of KM*. This important model remains one of the most studied and quoted descriptions of the complex knowledge management system. The foundation of the model is that each of the pillars represents a key element critical to knowledge management programs (Calabrese, 2000; Mohamed et al., 2004). Recent research further strengthened the authority of the model by statistically validating the existence of the four key elements and supporting their professed values and comparative significance. However, this important study did not consider all of the other representative models, and therefore it could not state categorically that the other models were not equally valid and valuable (Calabrese, 2000).

The second model originates from Europe and "aims to identify and support commonality in KM terminology, application, and implementation in Europe" (Weber et al., 2002, p. 1). This robust model offers a holistic and concise view of the major elements—much of which supports current North American academic and business views of knowledge management. The model not only reinforces the notion of system thinking but also follows traditional philosophies, based largely on Nonaka and APQC, in terms of the major components necessary for a successful implementation of knowledge management.

The U.S. Department of Navy, a world-renowned leader in public sector knowledge management, developed the final model. In 2002, under the leadership of Alex Bennet, the Department of the Navy was recognized as one of the most important knowledge management organizations in North America (Chatzkel, 2002). The Navy's model is based on their experience rather than academic research; however, the similarity to the academic models is striking and worthy of note. As knowledge management principles are relatively immature and continue to develop, one would be remiss to consider only the findings of academia when organizations such as the Navy have codified their extensive experience. In other academic fields, ignoring practical experience may be the norm and acceptable; however, oxymoronically, the study of experience must be a

	Technology	Leadership	Culture	Infrastructure	Organization	Process	Measures	Learning	Content
KM Pillars	✓	✓			✓			✓	
European Framework	✓	✓			✓	✓	✓		
Navy Balanced KM	✓		✓			✓		✓	✓
Enablers of Transfer	✓		✓	✓			✓		
Torii	✓	✓	✓			✓	✓		

Figure 3. Knowledge Management Models

part of the research of knowledge management. To ignore the lessons from real-world experience would be to deny the existence of tacit knowledge.

A review of the various knowledge management models suggests five enablers—Technology, Leadership, Culture, Measurement, and Process—are common in at least three of the five models. A further review of the remaining four enablers—Organization, Infrastructure, Learning, and Content—reveals that the essence of the latter cluster is embedded in the former group. For example, the designers of the *enablers of Transfer* model wrote, "Infrastructure includes the *transfer-specific mechanisms* put in to ensure best practices flow throughout the enterprise. These include technology, work processes, and networks of people" demonstrating the spirit of process is captured in what they call infrastructure (O'Dell et al., 1998, p. 107). Similarly, Dr. Stankosky opted to include the concept of process within the broad category of organization and placed culture within the leadership pillar. Thus, one may conclude that the core components of each model are extremely similar; arguably, the sole difference is semantics. To be sure, the precise titles are less important than the underlying concepts.

Torii—A Model of Knowledge Management Enablers

In this section, we introduce a new structure, the Torii, to describe the key enablers of knowledge management. We are unaware of others using this structure to describe knowledge transfer enablers; however, it seems that this traditional Japanese architectural structure is an excellent symbol to illustrate the enablers.

The Japanese often use a Torii as a portal to enter a sanctuary—for us the sanctuary is a knowledge environment. Normally the Japanese construct a Torii with two vertical bars supported by two or three horizontal bars. Key to the structural integrity of the Torii is the lowest horizontal bar, or Nuki, which binds the remaining horizontal and vertical bars. In the Torii, the trinity of Technology, Leadership, and Culture bonded by the Nuki of Process is illustrated. The highest bar in this Torii, known as the Kasagi, is Measurement. Like a real Torii, this highest bar is not essential to the structure's integrity; however, it plays an important role in ensuring the Torii is noticed and respected.

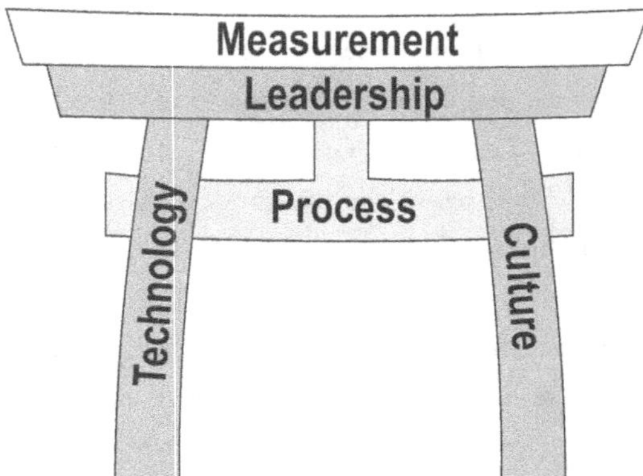

Figure 4. Torii, a New Model for the Enablers of Knowledge Management

Quantitative Research Results

The second stage of this investigation was to subject the theoretical construct to a quantitative analysis. To achieve this aim, one section of a recent survey instrument was dedicated to the component parts of the Torii model. Though exploratory in nature, the findings proved very interesting and therefore are worthy of review. The population under examination was the Canadian Public Service middle managers. The sampling technique used for this project was the snowball technique, which is not totally random. In reality, this sampling technique relies on motivated volunteers to complete the survey and solicit the support of their colleagues. This does not mean that this sample is not representative of the entire population; however, one must use care in generalizing the results too broadly. Ideally, additional research should be undertaken to corroborate these findings.

In order to moderate the risk of generalizing the research findings, the sample was compared to a large randomly selected sample, which is known to be representative of the population. The comparison sample was a Public Service Commission (PSC) online survey of Canadian government middle managers. From this finding, one may conclude that this sample is likely representative of the population. While acknowledging that bias exists in all studies utilizing the snowball sampling technique, the analysis of the demographic data indicates that the sample is not statistically different from the PSC survey indicating that one should be able to generalize the findings.

The online survey instrument included the statement *<blank> is an important enabler of knowledge management.* Of particular note was the discovery that 90% of respondents agreed or strongly agreed that Leadership is an important enabler of knowledge management. The importance of Leadership as an enabler was echoed in the qualitative comments, including "Projects that start today have the distinct advantage of all the advances in Information/Knowledge Management. However, the best tools available won't be of any use if Senior Management does not recognize the value of Knowledge Management" (Girard, 2005b, p. 5) or

> Starting knowledge management in an organization was one of the biggest challenges of my life. It involved adapting KM theory to the culture. Using a KM strategic document and a number of communicative means like workshops, published articles and a conference, we were able to move the organization in the direction of KM with the support of a KM champion. (Girard, 2005b, p. 5)

An intriguing discovery is that Culture was seen to be of equal importance as Technology. One respondent had very strong views on the relative importance of the two, especially if one compares the past to the future:

> In our organization, I believe that computers have deteriorated our information and knowledge systems. They have enabled individuals to develop and hoard their own systems and information in a fashion that would not be useful OR EVEN KNOWN to others in the organization. Great efforts have been made to provide and change culture to centralize information electronically, but is not consistently used and even less is it used to retrieve information that is pertinent to a current situation. Corporate Culture is the key to change. Then Measurement can be done more meaningfully and improvements in the organizational output realized. (Girard, 2005b, p. 5)

Buckman Laboratories—Knowledge in Action

We know that the Torii model and its components work fine in theory, but what about practice? The case that follows is certainly one of our favorites about knowledge in action. The case is not new—it dates back to the early 1990s; however, it is particularly useful because it chronicles one of the most effective knowledge revolutions to date. Equally important to note is that the organization remains one of the most renowned knowledge-empowered organizations on the planet; they have passed the test of time, so they must have done something right! We say this somewhat flippantly; however, the reality is that many of the so-called successes in the knowledge arena are short-lived or very isolated islands in large organizations. This is certainly not the case with the Buckman story. For a more detailed account of the Buckman story, we recommend Bob Buckman's book titled *Building a Knowledge-Driven Organization* (Buckman, 2004).

Buckman Laboratories is a chemical manufacturer and distributor headquartered in Memphis, Tennessee. They sell more than 1,000 different specialist chemical products around the world while employing over 1,200 people. However, they have become more renowned for their innovative corporate knowledge management network. Today, business leaders from some of the highest technology sectors visit Buckman Laboratories to learn about knowledge management.

This section examines, very briefly, the success of Buckman Laboratories with a view to determining how and why the company opted to invest in knowledge management to engage customers effectively. Many may see this case study as one about a new process, a new concept, or new technology; others will view this as a sociological study of corporate culture, and still others will see this as a story about leadership. All would be correct as this case study illustrates five essential enabling components to knowledge management—technology, leadership, culture, process, and measurement.

The transformation of Buckman Laboratories from a run-of-the-mill chemical company to a pioneering knowledge management company proves that innovative leaders may, virtually single-handedly, change the future of a company. We will see how one CEO's vision and determination revolutionized an industry by implementing an excellent knowledge management system. The lessons that one may learn from Buckman

Laboratories are many; however, the CEO's ability to gain and maintain employees' trust is the most significant leadership lesson learned.

In hindsight, the reasons for CEO Bob Buckman's interest in knowledge management may seem obvious; however, when the CEO began his quest for knowledge management in the early 1990s, the reasons were not so clear. In fact, it is due to pioneers like Bob Buckman that knowledge management is now one of the most critical corporate assets.

In 1992, Bob Buckman decided that his company required a *Cultural Revolution*. He decided to develop a system that would create a strategic advantage in a very competitive market in which his corporation operated. The corporate culture he envisaged was one where all employees shared knowledge to help the company rather than guarding the knowledge to use for personal gain. He realized that such a radical change would be difficult for his competitive, sales-oriented employees, but he knew it was the right thing to do for the corporation and its long-term success.

Bob Buckman desired a system where individual salespeople could rapidly exchange knowledge in a collaborative manner to effectively engage the customer. His vision was a system where these individuals would all add to and draw from the knowledge base. The individuals would work as a team and together they would be more powerful and more effective than the sum of the individuals. Having clearly articulated the *End State* of his proposal, the initial challenge was to determine how to put this revolutionary system into place. To implement his novel knowledge management system, Buckman and his team had to overcome two significant obstacles: technology and culture.

The first barrier was a technical one in that the communication infrastructure of the early 1990s was immature. To address this unacceptable situation, Buckman established a virtual Intranet on CompuServe, a public online system. Next, he leased laptop computers with modems for his entire sales force (Fulmer, 1999). This early example of a virtual private network was extremely innovative. Although this was a significant challenge for Buckman, we are fortunate that this impediment no longer exists. The lesson is that technological barriers require creative solutions. Organizations must not permit immature technology to stifle sound business practices. Undoubtedly, technology is an enabler of knowledge management; however, technology in its own right is not the panacea nor is technology necessarily essential for all knowledge management implementations. Unlike its distant cousin, information technology, knowledge management is truly an amalgamation of enablers. Nevertheless, in reality, most current knowledge management initiatives rely on technology to yield the results desired.

Buckman's second hurdle, which remains extremely relevant today, was how to convince his workforce to share valuable knowledge—in other words, how to develop trust. Buckman suggests, "What's happened here is 90% culture change" (Rifkin, 1996, p. 4). The saying, "knowledge is power," seems to be as true today as it was in the 17th century. Buckman believed "for knowledge-sharing to become a reality, you have to create a climate of trust in your organization" (Pan & Scarborough, 1999, p. 370). He knew his new philosophy of trust and knowledge sharing was right for his company, but how could he convince his sales staff to part with this precious asset—knowledge. In the past, the measure of success was sales, which relied on vital knowledge that one salesperson had and that others did not—this would have to change.

"Buckman believed strongly that employees who shared their knowledge would be the most influential and would be sought by others within the company" (Pan & Scarborough, 1999, p. 369). To ensure the success of his knowledge empowerment scheme, Buckman offered incentives for those who participated, but he also made it clear there would be few opportunities for those who opted not to contribute. Focusing on the positive, Buckman awarded the highest contributors with rewards such as computers and trips. He developed a code of ethics that stressed the importance of individuals, and he worked with the sales force to develop a new compensation plan that balanced sales with collaboration.

By achieving such a fundamental cultural change, he realized the strategic advantage that he desired. This excellent lesson is not unique to Buckman as collaboration, trust, and mutual respect—in other words, *corporate culture*—are key ingredients to all effective knowledge management implementations. Bob Buckman's ability to revolutionize his company's work practices and to develop a trusting environment speaks volumes on his leadership ability. Influencing commissioned-focused sales representatives to give up their hottest commodity—knowledge—is an amazing feat. Change at the best of times is difficult, but to change the basic philosophy from *knowledge is power* to one of cooperation is no small task and would have overwhelmed a less gifted leader.

Buckman Laboratories are world renowned as leaders in knowledge management. This relatively unassuming chemical company developed a pioneering concept of team building, trust, and collaboration. By overcoming major technical and cultural obstacles, CEO Bob Buckman initiated a vast revolution that ensured that all employees shared information to help the company, rather than guarding the information to use for personal gain. Clearly, Buckman was a CEO with vision and one who very successfully influenced his team to change their working environment.

This trusting milieu has empowered the workforce and has created a strategic advantage in a very competitive market in which his corporation operates. Buckman's aim was to increase the percentage of his workforce effectively engaged with clientele. After the transition, the salespeople at the front line, dealing with customers, rose by 300% (Rifkin, 1996). Bob Buckman developed the concept of treating knowledge as a critical corporate asset. The most gratifying recognition of his success is the number of companies trying to emulate his work. We have seen how an innovative, persuasive, and stalwart leader may guide their organization to success. CEO Bob Buckman is quoted regularly as a knowledge management guru—and he is—however, we should also acknowledge and quote Buckman as an astonishing leader. Only someone such as Bob Buckman, who attained such a degree of excellence in both the leadership and technical worlds, could have possibly implemented such an ingenious concept. Perhaps someday soon we will witness a number of corporate leaders trying to emulate Buckman's leadership, in addition to his knowledge management techniques.

In many ways, the process enabler is the glue that binds the trinity of technology, leadership, and culture. The trinity, which we term the TLC of KM, must be present for knowledge management to be effective; nevertheless, process is the enabler that spawns value. Only through process may organizations truly achieve the competitive advantage they seek. Buckman understood this notion well and demanded the development of procedures that provided his sales force with the knowledge they needed at the point of contact with customers. With on-the-spot access to the combined knowledge of all employees, the frontline salespeople were able to make accurate, informed, and timely decisions to help their customers. According to Buckman, this process of making the knowledge of all employees available to the entire organization narrowed the gap between his company and his customers (O'Dell, Davenport, & Croy, 1997).

A second example of process at Buckman was titled the *Case History* system. This electronic knowledge base codified the challenges identified by the sales force and their suggested solutions. This explicit knowledge transfer process permitted the frontline sales team to query quickly the system to determine how others had responded to challenging or unique questions from customers. In the first decade, the knowledge base was populated with nearly 2,500 real cases, allowing salespeople to resolve problems more effectively and efficiently than ever before (O'Dell et al., 1997).

The *raison d'être* for Buckman's cultural revolution was to deploy knowledge at the point of sale. By putting knowledge in the field, at the point of sale, Buckman believed he could add value that his competition could not accomplish. Clearly, it was essential to measure somehow the success of this new initiative in order to determine if the new business practice was achieving the desired results.

For Buckman Laboratories, the preeminent measure was the proportion of the workforce directly engaged with their customers. In 1979, before Buckman conceived his revolutionary concept, only 16% of his workforce was at the front line dealing with customers. By 1996, he had tripled that number to about 50% and had plans in place to increase the number to 80% effectively engaged with customers (Fulmer, 1999; Rifkin, 1996). A second measure of their knowledge-sharing program was based on the number of new products as a percentage of sales. In a decade, this effectiveness percentage raised from 14% to 34.6% (O'Dell et al., 1997).

Knowledge management will be one way that leaders of the future may conquer the many challenges confronting their organizations. However, to ensure the best return on their knowledge investment, one must understand and apply the enablers of knowledge management. The Torii knowledge model, which includes the enablers of Technology, Leadership, Culture, Process, and Measurement, may go some way in ensuring organizations derive maximum benefit. Some say the model is too simple—we consider this a compliment!

Remember Bob Buckman

Bob Buckman was a pioneer in the domain of knowledge management. His transformation of a run-of-the-mill chemical company into one of the most respected knowledge organizations was a near-herculean feat. Learning from his successes, other organizational leaders are able to replicate, or at least emulate, his achievements.

Now You Know . . .

- The enablers of knowledge management are technology, leadership, and culture.
- Organizational leaders must decide how success will be measured.
- Knowledge processes may include socialization, externalization, combination, and internalization.
- **Combination** is the transfer of explicit to explicit knowledge. Through the process of codification, one person may document specific knowledge into some form of repository so that many others may access knowledge. An organization developing and formalizing best practices is a classic example of transferring explicit knowledge. Equally common is the creation of new knowledge by combining previously documented explicit knowledge.
- **Externalization** is the transfer of tacit knowledge to the explicit form. For example, one may wish to articulate or externalize the highly personal knowledge of a master artisan into an explicit form that is easier to formalize or document.
- **Internalization** is the transfer of explicit knowledge to the tacit form. The premise is knowledge creation through an amalgamation of codified explicit knowledge and fuzzy tacit knowledge. Consider the master artisan who educates himself in the sciences and through this education and his intuition is able to develop a better way to produce his craft.
- **Socialization** is the transfer of tacit to tacit knowledge. Through social interaction, people may gain highly personal

and difficult-to-formalize knowledge. One of the best examples is the apprentice shadowing the master artisan. Almost through osmosis, the young journeyperson learns the craft of the master. He or she will probably not understand the scientific principles underlying the master's skill, but through socialization, the student slowly gains the knowledge required to replicate the teacher.

PART 2

Leading Today's Knowledge Workers

CHAPTER 4

Simple Ideas That Work in Complex Environments

I believe what I said yesterday.
I don't know what I said,
but I know what I think, and, well,
I assume it's what I said.

—Former U.S. Secretary of Defense Donald Rumsfeld

A time-honored consultant's tactic is to ask executives what keeps them awake at night. The answer to this simple question often provides a clue as to the burning platform from which the seasoned consultant may offer advice on how to solve the executive's problems. This does not always work, of course. John once witnessed a very experienced leader answer the question by saying, "My dog, my dog keeps me awake at night." At first, he was taken back. John thought he must be kidding . . . but he wasn't!

In this chapter, we will review a series of challenges facing the baby-boomer generation of executives and some common solutions with a view to answering the question, Is knowledge power? We will start this exploration by examining why many executives crave the facts. Next, we will consider the rather bizarre concept of unknown unknowns. Along the way, we will explore some time-tested solutions that have helped baby-boomer executives create knowledge-empowered organizations. To navigate the many success stories—and some not so successful stories—we will use Nonaka's SECI model as a map.

Just the Facts, Please

Let us face it, executives are busy people, and they do not have time for extra words, especially pronouns. How many times have you heard an executive say, "I just want the facts"? But do you as an executive really want the facts? Remember that in a previous chapter data was defined *as a set of discrete, objective facts about events.* We suggest that from a management perspective two features are worthy of note. The first of these was data is the lowest level in the value chain and by itself is not very beneficial. Arguably, too much data exists and until or unless managers transform this data into information, it is simply occupying valuable space.

So why is it that executives crave data? If they buy into the concepts of knowledge management, then one would think that they should prefer having access to processed data, which many people call information or maybe even knowledge. Recall Peter Drucker's description, "Information is data endowed with relevance and purpose" (1988, p. 46), which seems to imply that senior managers would wish this relevant entity (information) rather than the raw form (data). However, no matter how many times they remind themselves of this concept, the executives continue to say, "I want the facts." Well, maybe the answer is to give them facts, but in a way that can make a difference.

Previously, we suggested that combination was the preferred way for Westerners or occidentals to create knowledge. Some would suggest that such a statement is a hasty generalization, and we admit that could be true. However, before admitting defeat we would like to know how many times have you heard an executive say, "Can you run the numbers on that?" or "What happens if you combine that data with last quarter's data?" or many similar questions. The reality is, we would argue, that many of us like to create new knowledge by combining two or more sources of explicit data. We will use this idea of combination to begin our examination of knowledge management in action.

In the first chapter, we critiqued the Tofflers for using a broad definition of knowledge. We argued that it is important to be able to differentiate between the three terms and then we went on, at great length, to describe the difference between the three terms. Although we believe it is important to understand the difference, especially from an academic point of view, we know that when a tough decision must be made the last thing an executive is considering is the difference between three related concepts. What executives need, and need now, is whatever nugget will help them make a decision.

One of the real problems with the pyramid concept of data, information, and knowledge is that the boundaries are not clear. What is data to one person may be knowledge to another. At the end of the day, executives crave whatever is needed to make a decision; they do not worry about the nomenclature. Verna Allee, author of several excellent knowledge management books, reminds us that "fuzzy boundaries create innovation" (Allee, 2003, p. 4). This phase was the catalyst for a new model to describe the relationship between data management, information management, and knowledge management. Rather than focus on whether a particular tool, tactic, or technique should be labeled as a data management, information management, or knowledge management, the model suggests that a continuum exists. By eliminating strict boundaries, which are often difficult to define, the model focuses on outputs rather than preconceived categorizations.

Creating Knowledge With Data

Data mining is an excellent example of this concept in action. Some would argue that data mining is data-dependent and therefore a data management tool. Others argue that data mining was not possible until powerful information technology systems were available to take deep dives into the vast stores of data and therefore it must be an information management tool. Still others contend that data mining is clearly knowledge management. At the end of the day, the executive who makes a vital decision because of a particular process is more concerned with the result than the label.

Consider the following example of data mining in action. According to NCR Corporation, one of its divisions (Teradata)

> pioneered the field of data mining by looking at sales data from a retailer and discovering that in the evening hours, beer and diapers are often purchased together. This relationship, called a data mining affinity, captured the imagination of industry watchers, spawning a legend that has been recounted hundreds of times and is frequently cited as the textbook example of data mining. (Michael, 2002)

Much has been written about this example of data mining in action. Many of the articles describe the technology used to discover this relationship while others describe the mathematics used to develop the algorithms.

However, the aspect of most interest to us is what the retailer did with this valuable information. Imagine that you are at the helm of a large retail operation and you are presented with the findings of this experimental research. At an executive meeting, the vice president of sales, supported by the chief information officer, describe their findings. They tell a story that every Friday evening, most people who purchase beer also purchase diapers. They have the data to prove it; each and every Friday there is a very clear relationship between beer sales and diapers sales.

The question is, what do you do armed with this *knowledge*? Most executives would consider how they could use this *knowledge* to create a competitive advantage. They would realize the value of this *knowledge* is time limited. In other words, once their competitors discover the relationship, the value of the *knowledge* will be diminished. Before answering the question, how many executives would stop to ask the question, Am I dealing with data, information, or knowledge? None. Well, no executive who wants to remain competitive would pause to answer such a trivial question. The reality is executives are not concerned with the nomenclature, but rather with the results.

So what really happened? What did the retailer do? This is where the urban myth part of the story starts. Many tales have been told about the unnamed retailer—so many that many skeptics suggest the whole event may not have existed. Like many great stories, the most important thing is the story must be believable; it does not have to be true, but it does have to be believable. But more about stories later.

When John shares this story of data mining in action with his Master's level knowledge management students, he asks the students what they think happened. Predictably, there is a group of students that suggest that beer and diapers would be put together in some convenient location, perhaps near the front of the store. A second group usually emerges arguing that the beer should be put at one end of the store with the diapers at the far end. Some continue by suggesting that we could strategically locate other convenience items along the route. Each of these courses of action seems reasonable.

Many of the students are surprised when John suggests the CEO decided to do nothing. He continues by saying that the CEO was very impressed with the discovery and that she complimented the VP Sales and CIO. After describing how valuable knowledge this was, the CEO announces that the company will not make any changes because of the revelation. The CEO continues by saying that she believes that encouraging the purchase of beer and diapers was not something she wished to pursue. She finishes her discourse by saying, "Knowledge is power—having the supporting data to make this decision was extremely valuable."

The most important point in this story is that the CEO had the data, information, or knowledge (whatever you wish to call it) that she needed to make the decision. We can debate the decision, but at the end of the day, the most important issue is that the CEO had what she needed to make an important corporate decision. Knowledge management is about making sure that senior executives know what they need to know to make the decisions that they must make.

Some people question the authenticity of the beer and diapers story. In fact, many of John's students ask for other examples of data mining in action. One of the challenges with the beer and diapers example is that it took place in 1991. Correctly, graduate students are very skeptical of events that were pioneered when they were in grade school and are still being highlighted as the way of the future. In fact, we encourage this skepticism of ideas that remain immature after a decade and half.

Although many people, students and executives alike, appreciate how data mining could be used to create a competitive advantage, they seek real examples of the technique that have demonstrated and measurable results. Anticipating this question, John goes to class prepared to tell another compelling story about data mining.

The lead in to the story goes something like this. What do you think the Wal-Mart corporation rushes to its own stores in areas where a hurricane is predicted? The usual answers are flashlights, water, batteries, and the like. Most students are surprised to hear that Wal-Mart ships strawberry-flavored Kellogg's Pop-Tarts to areas threatened by hurricanes. The follow-on question is usually, Why would they ship Pop-Tarts? The answer is very simple; Wal-Mart regularly mines the trillions of bytes of data they collect from consumers looking for relationships. Perhaps more astonishing is what they find. For example, Wal-Mart discovers a sevenfold sales of Pop-Tarts ahead of hurricanes (Hays, 2004).

Some students will dig a little deeper and demand to know why. Why is it that consumers like to purchase Pop-Tarts ahead of a storm? The short answer is no one is quite sure. There are likely marketing students across the country trying to answer this exact question. They are busy creating consumer surveys that will be used to collect data that will be analyzed, and with a bit of luck they will be able to explain this heretofore-unpredictable consumer activity. In two or three years, we will know the answer to this question.

But wait, can we compete with Wal-Mart or other data miners if we study the problem for 2 years and then we are in a position to explain why consumers did something 2 years ago? Of course not. Wal-Mart calls their data-mining effort *predictive technology;* others are calling it a *data-driven weapon* illustrating the warlike atmosphere of retailing today. By the time others explain why people bought Pop-Tarts during Hurricane Frances, Wal-Mart will be predicting, very accurately, what consumers will purchase during the next disaster (Hays, 2004).

Before leaving the Wal-Mart example, there is one more issue that should be addressed. We are often asked what else sells well ahead of a hurricane. According to Wal-Mart, another pre-hurricane top seller is, well you guessed it, beer. Therefore, a cunning retailer might assume that diapers should also sell well!

Combination—It's Not Always Good!

The two stories of data mining in action are excellent examples of what Nonaka termed combination in the SECI model. By combining two or more pieces of explicit data, we have created new knowledge. In these cases, the knowledge appears to have created a competitive advantage, which of course is a good thing. You may recall that earlier we were quite critical of Westerners' use of combination as a knowledge-creation technique and now we are promoting it as a way to create a competitive advantage.

As is often the case, there are good and bad examples of many tools and techniques. The basis of our criticism is that many Westerners believe that simply combining two pieces of explicit knowledge will ensure new knowledge is created. Let us share a couple of examples of combination not really adding value—both of which are very close to home!

At a recent knowledge management conference, the keynote speaker suggested that little new or interesting had been published in the knowledge management domain for some time. The speaker, an author himself, lamented about the repetition that is commonplace in many recent books. He argued that the study of knowledge management has not advanced much since the seminal works of Nonaka and Takeuchi (*The Knowledge-Creating Company*), Davenport and Prusak (part of Operation Enduring Freedom.), and perhaps a couple others. His underlying point was that authors were not creating new knowledge but rather just repackaging the same old knowledge. In other words, the combination of explicit knowledge did not necessarily create new knowledge. Ironically, he was at the conference to launch a new knowledge management book!

Not that long ago, our son, John, was serving aboard a Canadian warship in the Persian Gulf, as part of Operation *Enduring Freedom*. His ship was part of a larger formation known as the USS *George Washington* battlegroup, aptly named because the lead ship in the group was the aircraft carrier USS *George Washington*. All total, there were six ships in this futuristic flotilla, each of which were in constant contact with the mother ship. Gone are the days where ships pass in the night without notice. Gone are the days when ships rely on semaphore or even radios to stay in contact. In fact, today's modern warships are one of the best examples of virtual collaboration in action. Each ship is inextricably connected to the remainder of the flotilla.

At the personal level, technology played an important role in ensuring our son was able to stay connected with his friends and family back home. In modern navies, this homeward-bound connection may be as important as the interconnectedness of the operational ships. Though it may be true that Napoleon's armies could "march on food," soldiers, sailors, and airmen and women today are probably more concerned about staying connected than they are about the quality or quantity of their food. If you are in doubt, simply ask a soldier if he or she would rather have a MRE (meal ready to eat, which is actually an oxymoron) or a 5-minute phone call home.

One day, during his 6-month "cruise" in the Persian Gulf, our son decided to explore other opportunities in the military. Although we are not entirely certain what triggered this sudden quest for knowledge, we were very impressed that modern satellite technology allowed him to search the vast stores of data on the Defence Wide Area Network. He was able to access, almost instantly, all the information he wanted to decide what military occupation would be of most interest to him. He was able to read fact sheets and download and watch videos that described each job. Essentially, he had access to everything that would have been available to him if he was back home—very impressive.

He also had access to vast volumes of regulations that explain the process for changing careers. As you can imagine, it is a very bureaucratic process to change careers in the military. There are many forms to fill out and many deadlines to meet. As he continued to navigate through this maze of *knowledge*, he began to trip on contradictions. He found different dates, different processes, and different approval authorities. The more he searched, the more contradictions he found. Soon it became clear that he would not be able to rely on the data he was finding—it was simply impossible to determine which documents were up-to-date and which ones were dangerous old relics taking up valuable space.

At the end of the day, our son contacted us for help. He knew that we would know someone who would have the *real* knowledge he needed. Indeed, he was correct, and after just a couple of telephone calls, we were able to connect with the person who knew the real procedures. This is a great example of how knowledge flows in many organizations. Frequently it makes more sense to find a person who knows what you need to know rather than search volumes of uncontrolled content on corporate intranets.

This story illustrates several crucial points. First, organizations should have procedures for content management and digital asset management; in short, someone should own all data and be responsible to maintain it. However, technology alone will not suffice. Often people prefer to connect with other people rather than the data. To satisfy this want, organizations should consider investing in systems to facilitate this human-to-human connection such as *yellow pages* or *expert location systems*, both of which will be explored in more detail later in the book.

Stories of Simple Ideas That Work in Complex Environments

For several years, we have had the great pleasure of speaking to groups of organizational leaders about knowledge management. Specifically, we speak about how leaders may reap the benefits of creating and sharing organizational knowledge. This journey has taken us to destinations across the United States and Canada as well as Europe, Asia, South America, Africa, and Australia. In fact, Antarctica is the only continent where we have not spoken about knowledge management—we await an invitation!

Over the years, our talks have changed. Initially, we spoke about rather complex cognitive theories with the hope that folks in the audience would take our *words of wisdom* and single-handedly transform their organizations. After many sessions of watching yet another audience grin politely as we delivered our sermon, we realized that we were contributing to one of the common themes of our talks—*information overload*.

As it turns out, much of what we were talking about was simply *lost in the translation*. At first, we wondered if it was the audiences because it certainly could not be us! After each presentation, we would spend hours answering e-mails from individuals with questions such as "I really enjoyed your talk; however, I am not really sure how to implement the ideas you were discussing. Do you have any examples of these ideas in action?" After many nights of responding to similar questions, we realized (finally) that we were making the whole thing seem very complicated.

We began to respond to questions with short stories that illustrated the point we were trying to make. Most of these stories were based on real organizations—although we would often change the names to protect the innocent, like Joe Friday from Dragnet. One day we had an epiphany: Why wait until after the presentation to share these stories? We decided to transform our talks into a series of stories that explained the (unnecessarily) complicated theories we were describing. The rest, as they say, is history.

This was the genesis of a presentation titled *Simple Ideas That Work in Complex Environments*. The premise was rather simple (pun intended): to describe some ideas, many of which were grounded in complicated cognitive theories, that seemed to work in complex environments. What, you may ask, is a complex environment? We opted to use Merriam-Webster's definition for complex: "a group of obviously related units of which the degree and nature of the relationship is imperfectly known" ("complex," 2009). This terse definition describes so many of the organizations in which we have worked, studied, or consulted. The final clause seemed to be key: "the degree and nature of the relationship is imperfectly known."

The data-mining stories in the previous section, as well as the stories that follow, are from the collection of the stories that we use in our talks. The anthology includes original stories, classic stories, stories based on television commercials, stories that have helped guide great organizations, and stories from exceptional leaders (such as the one below). Although the origin of each story is very different, we believe that they all share the common theme of simplifying complex environments. Of course, you are the real judge; let us know what you think. Many of the stories have transcended the boundaries of our talks—we now use them in a variety of venues including graduate and undergraduate management classes, corporate training events, and consulting. Three of our favorites are below.

Unknown Unknowns—Gibberish or Wisdom?

The Plain English Campaign is a United Kingdom–based organization that describes itself as "an independent pressure group fighting for public information to be written in plain English" ("Plain English Campaign," 2006). Annually, the Plain English Campaign presents a variety of awards focusing on the use of English. One of their awards is titled the *Foot in Mouth*, which they present to a public figure for a baffling quote. In 2003, the recipient of the *Foot in Mouth* award was former U.S. Defense Secretary Donald Rumsfeld for saying the following during a Pentagon press conference on February 12, 2002:

> As we know, there are known knowns; there are things we know we know. We also know there are known unknowns; that is to say we know there are some things we do not know. But there are also unknown unknowns—the ones we don't know we don't know. And if one looks throughout the history of our country and other free countries, it is the latter category that tend to be the difficult ones. ("DoD News Briefing—Secretary Rumsfeld and Gen. Myers," 2002)

Say what? What do you mean there are known knowns, known unknowns, and unknown unknowns? This sounds like gibberish at best or perhaps just pure nonsense. Many journalist poked fun at Donald Rumsfeld, and a series of Internet sites emerged to document the *poetry* of Rumsfeld. Surely, the Secretary misspoke or was misquoted. In fact, nothing could be further from the truth as Donald Rumsfeld very concisely described a major complex management challenge. The challenge is best illustrated using a 2 x 2 matrix:

<table>
<tr><td>UNKNOWN
KNOWNS</td><td>UNKNOWN
UNKNOWNS</td></tr>
<tr><td>KNOWN
KNOWNS</td><td>KNOWN
UNKNOWNS</td></tr>
</table>

Figure 5. Rumsfeld's Unknown Unknowns

The point that Secretary Rumsfeld so eloquently articulated in just 20 seconds has since been the subject of a variety of articles and book chapters. Take for example Alex and David Bennet's chapter titled "Exploring the Unknown" in their book *Organizational Survival in the New World: The Intelligent Complex Adaptive System.* This chapter focuses on "how do we identify things that we don't know we don't know" (Bennet & Bennet, 2004). This is exactly what Rumsfeld was suggesting. If we know that we do not know something, then we can develop a plan to find out more. Likewise, if we do not know that we know something, then again we can develop a plan to find the missing link. Both of these issues are dealt with during external and internal scanning, competitive intelligence, and the like.

The 2 x 2 matrix is a useful way to categorize the challenges confronting many originations. Unfortunately, most leaders focus on the easy bits: things they know and things that they know that they do not know. Many organizations ignore the upper right-hand quadrant—the unknown unknowns—because it is just too difficult. Perhaps some ignore this quadrant because they do not know what to do. A very good example of a time-tested tool to conquer this quadrant is data mining, as we discussed earlier in this chapter. That said, to some degree, the avoidance of the upper right-hand quadrant is a symptom of the *not on my watch syndrome.* Many leaders do not wish to dig too deep into the unknown unknowns because it is uncharted territory. Equally concerning is the fear that discovering unknown unknowns will expose a corporate Achilles heel. Then what would we do?

The other quadrant that often creates anxiety is the upper left or unknown knowns quadrant. One of our favorite stories about this quadrant features a large technology company. The story is loosely based on a real company, but given we embellished a few parts to make our point, we must declare it is a fictional company—let us call them IQ. IQ is a well-known brand that for many years operated with a divisional organization structure. Once a year, each of the divisional vice presidents were afforded the opportunity to brief the Board of Directors on their plans for the future. This rare occasion was seen to be a time when senior executives could describe the next big thing that would provide IQ with a competitive advantage.

One year, the printer division's vice president was extremely excited about his time with the Board. He was sure the directors would agree that his new idea, a printer that could also scan, would be a history-making innovative product, a must-have for many small businesses. The R & D arm of the printer division had been working secretly on the project for some time. After investing considerable resources, their prototype was ready to be showcased to the Board. They were very proud of their clandestine operation; it was quite a coup that none of the technology press had picked up on their work.

Finally, the big day arrived. The vice president was waiting patiently in the anteroom reviewing his presentation. Suddenly, an unprecedented level of applause from inside the boardroom interrupted his thoughts. Shortly afterward the vice president of the scanner division emerged, smiling, and clearly happy with her performance in the room. The printer executive politely asked his colleague why the Board erupted into applause. After a short pause, she replied, "I just showed the Board our prototype for the next big thing . . . a scanner that can also print." Needless to say, the printer executive was no longer excited about briefing the Board.

The moral of the story is that a *need to know* culture, which is commonplace in many technology companies, does not facilitate knowledge sharing. Here is a case where senior executives did not share, let alone collaborate on the project. Imagine if the two divisions shared resources and knowledge to design the printer scanner. Regrettably, many organizations fall victim to the unknown knowns because they do not foster a collaborative environment with a need to share philosophy.

We Have a Problem!

The nightmare scenario for many executives is a call in the night that begins with the words, "We have a problem!" Almost certainly one of the most famous problems was in April 1970 when astronaut Jack Swigert, aboard *Apollo 13*, radioed Houston and said the famous, but oft misquoted, phrase "Houston, we've had a problem!" Fortunately, most management decisions are not life and death as was the case with *Apollo 13*.

Nevertheless, organizations must be prepared for crisis decision making. It is too late to consider what values are important to an organization when crises present themselves. The recent and spectacular failures of large corporations seem to indicate that many corporate leaders are ill prepared or unwilling to deal with unanticipated tribulations. However, there are a few great examples of organizations whose management teams internalize core values in quiet times so that they are prepared for catastrophic events.

In 1943, when General Robert Wood Johnson penned "Our Credo" for Johnson & Johnson, he had no idea just how important this short passage would become. He had no idea how his carefully crafted words would help the leaders of the next generation. The Credo has been changed, ever so slightly, since 1943; however, most of the changes have been in language and not in substance or spirit. The Credo begins by stating, "We believe our first responsibility is to the doctors, nurses and patients, to mothers and fathers and all others who use our products and services. In meeting their needs everything we do must be of high quality." The Credo continues with some guiding principles and then concludes by stating, "When we operate according to these principles, the stockholders should realize a fair return" (see http://tinyurl.com/c7rtfa for the complete text of the one-page Credo).

The Credo proved its worth when some malefactors infected some Tylenol with cyanide in 1982. According Lawrence G. Foster, vice president of public relations for Johnson & Johnson, "The Credo served the company better than any crisis management plan could have" (Foster, 1983). Based on the Credo, the Johnson & Johnson managers knew what to do. However, how can a 40-year-old one-page document help managers make decisions? The answer is that everyone in Johnson & Johnson is aware of the Credo and its importance. It is more than words on a paper. It is more than just some poster hanging in conference rooms. It has become synonymous with Johnson & Johnson, and all managers know what it means.

All too often, executives go through the motions of developing a mission, vision, and values so that they may be proudly displayed in offices. To many, this is a paper exercise that does not really change the price of fish. Johnson & Johnson's Credo is NOT simply a paper exercise. Johnson & Johnson's Credo is a guiding document that has passed the test of time, and it is an excellent example of what Nonaka termed internalization.

A Day to Remember

For many of us, August 14, 2003, is a date we will remember. That was the day that some 50 million Americans and Canadians witnessed a blackout across the Northeast portion of the North American continent. On that hot August day, we were living in Ottawa, Canada's capital. Brownouts, a temporary reduction in electric power, are relatively common in Ontario during the summer and although local blackouts are not unheard of, they are quite rare. The "usual suspect" in these cases is high summer temperatures, which in turn cause people to crank up their air conditioners. Invariably this puts a strain on the power grid and sometimes the result is a brownout or very occasionally a blackout.

We knew this day was different when we received a telephone call from our daughter, Terri-Lynn. At the time, she was a Human Resource Associate at Wal-Mart in Ottawa. We were not surprised when she told us that her store was using emergency power as our house was without electricity and it was only about 2 miles from her office. What really surprised us was when she said that she had just spoken to a Toronto store and it, too, was experiencing a blackout. Her colleague stated that the entire metropolitan Toronto area was in the dark. All of a sudden, the situation changed. How could Ottawa (population 800,000) and Toronto (population 2,500,000) be without electricity?

We turned on a battery-powered radio to discover that New York and Detroit were also without power. If the news reports were true, then at least 15 million people were in the dark, maybe even more. How could this be? Not surprisingly, there was talk of malicious attacks. This seemed plausible. Now what?

Well, in hindsight we now know that this was not caused by a targeted attacked on the North American infrastructure but rather an unfortunate, though predictable, shutdown designed to protect the grid. The real question becomes, What should we do to ensure this never happens again? One way is to conduct an After Action Review, or AAR, which considers four questions:

1. What was supposed to happen?
2. What happened?
3. What is the difference?
4. What should we do to improve?

The U.S. Army designed the AAR process more than two decades ago. The premise is simple—how can we learn from our mistakes to ensure we do not repeat the same mistakes? We like to think about it as a scheme that encourages making "new" mistakes rather than the same old ones. Of course, for the U.S. Army it is much more serious than avoiding old mistakes because an avoidable mistake may be dire—it may involve the loss of life of a brave American soldier and we must avoid that at all costs.

Today many organizations are benefiting from the outstanding work of the U.S. Army; organizations across the United States and around the world have implemented AARs to ensure they make new mistakes. AARs are a powerful concept for creating and transferring organizational knowledge; however, like many management processes, they must be implemented with care.

Often it is a good idea to have a trained facilitator help organizations learn the craft of AARs. Once AARs become commonplace, they should be conducted by internal managers. Remember, AARs are not about assigning or implying blame, but rather, AARs are about making sure that organizations do not repeat the same mistakes. AAR sessions should be short and positive. Do NOT allow the sessions to turn into a witch hunt or a finger-pointing exercise. AARs are a very good example of what Nonaka termed Externalization. By the way, it turns out the cause of the blackout of 2003 was likely due to trees not being trimmed as they should have been.

Remember Donald Rumsfeld

The poetry of former Secretary Donald Rumsfeld is frequently mocked. Regrettably, the mockers of his words of wisdom often miss the point and the real lessons are lost in the laughter. Rumsfeld's unknown unknowns speech is one that should not be mocked, ignored, or forgotten. Some executives will recognize the brilliance of his words; the most successful executives will heed his advice and dedicate resources to learning about unknown unknowns. Data mining is a useful tool in this quest.

Now You Know . . .

- Executives frequently crave the *facts*; however, it is often better to provide knowledge that will support decision making.
- Data mining is a powerful technique for discovering rather bizarre but very useful data anomalies.
- Leaders should ensure that the content on organizational intranets, portals, and the like is not out of date.
- Thinking about unknown unknowns may well reap benefits.
- Johnson & Johnson's Credo provides an excellent example of knowledge internalization in action.
- An After Action Review, or AAR, is a post-event knowledge capture process that considers four questions:

    1. What was supposed to happen?
    2. What happened?
    3. What is the difference?
    4. What should we do to improve?

CHAPTER 5

Do You Really Want to Know What You Know?

Yu, shall I teach you what knowledge is? When you know a thing, to hold that you know it; and when you do not know a thing, to allow that you do not know it;—this is knowledge.

—Confucius, *The Analects*, 2:17

The premise of this book is that, in general, building organizational memories creates a competitive advantage. More specifically, we argue that if executives know what their organizations knew in the past, they will be better prepared to make well-informed decisions. In turn, these knowledge-based decisions will ensure the organization is better at whatever it is that it does. In short, understanding the past will help guide organizations into the future.

There are a growing number of proponents of exactly the opposite principle. In other words, they suggest that letting go of the past may well be the most profitable route to the future. These researchers argue, convincingly, that focusing on the past may stifle innovation and may even prevent corporate executives from thinking out of the box. This interesting assertion seems to counter the main claim of this book; however, as one explores the realm of organizational forgetting, it quickly becomes evident that this idea complements, not contradicts, the building of organizational memories.

The aim of this chapter is to consider how the tenets of organizational forgetting make possible the building of organizational memories. The literature is rich in research in this domain, and the scope of our book precludes an extensive review (de Holan & Phillips, 2004; Govindarajan & Trimble, 2006; Kwiatkowski, Duncan, & Shimmin, 2006). Rather, this terse review of organizational forgetting will focus on the four components to organizational forgetting articulated by Pablo de Holan and his colleagues (de Holan, Phillips, & Lawrence, 2004). After exploring the counterintuitive construct of organizational forgetting, we will consider two related issues. The first are virtual memories, an annoying reality of the modern society that has no business at the office. Finally, we will examine in more detail the notion of information anxiety, which was introduced earlier.

Accidental Forgetting

According to de Holan et al., there are two modes of forgetting, *intentional* or *accidental*. Likewise, they suggest there are two sources of knowledge, *from existing stock* and *newly innovated*. Combining the two premises results in a matrix that describes the four categories of organizational forgetting that de Holan et al. discovered in their research (de Holan et al., 2004). The four quadrants (memory decay, failure to capture, unlearning, and avoiding bad habits) of this matrix provide an excellent framework to consider how managers may wish to consider the application of organizational forgetting.

Memory decay is the accidental loss of existing organizational knowledge. Earlier we defined knowledge as "a fluid mix of framed experience, values, contextual information, expert insight that provides a framework for evaluating and incorporating new experiences and information" (Davenport & Prusak, 1998, p. 5). From an organizational point of view, managers must consider the impact or consequences of failing to maintain the existing store of experience, values, contextual information, and expert insight.

As Davenport and Prusak so eloquently remind us, "In organizations, it [knowledge] often becomes embedded not only in documents or repositories but also in organizational routines, processes, practices, and norms" (p. 5). Therefore, we must consider both the explicit and tacit forms of knowledge that may be accidentally forgotten. In terms of building organizational memories, we should consider the future value, positive or negative, of forgetting what was once known. Consider this extreme example of organizational memory loss:

> One horrible day 1,600 years ago, the wisdom of many centuries went up in flames. The great library in Alexandria burned down, a catastrophe at the time and a symbol for all ages of the vulnerability of human knowledge. The tragedy forced scholars to

grope to reconstruct a grand literature and science that once lay neatly cataloged in scrolls. (Linden, 1991)

Perhaps one of the best modern examples of memory decay is the finding that the National Aeronautics and Space Administration (NASA) has *lost* the knowledge necessary to travel to the moon. It appears that NASA lost the only set of blueprints for a critical component of the rocket used to carry astronauts to the moon. However, the loss of this explicit knowledge is not the only problem, as some observers suggest that even if NASA had the codified knowledge to build another rocket, no one possesses the tacit knowledge necessary to fly the Saturn rocket (Petch, 2001).

In his book *Lost Knowledge*, author David DeLong discusses the drivers of lost knowledge and suggests that NASA's loss may have been the result of an aging population and the complexity of their knowledge (2004). Clearly, the former was part of the problem in the moon example as most of the engineers, scientists, and indeed astronauts involved in the 1960s and 1970s Apollo project have long since retired.

Managers must start looking forward rather than backward. Of course, there will be retirements—there will also be deaths, terminations, transfers, and a variety of exiting of employees and their knowledge. Although the spike in retirements associated with baby boomers is making executives take notice, the reality is not a new problem, nor is it a challenge that will diminish in the future.

Described as "failing to incorporate new knowledge into the broader organizational memory," *failure to capture* is the second category of accidental organizational forgetting (de Holan et al., 2004, p. 48). Much like memory decay, this is an unintentional act and once managers are aware of the consequences of not capturing the knowledge, then steps may be taken to remedy the situation. To a large degree, the solution to both the memory decay and failure to capture challenges lies in a solid knowledge management strategy as described later in the book. Given the unintentional nature of this malady, a focused knowledge management plan will ensure that the necessary steps are taken to guard his corporate resource.

Intentional Forgetting

Unlike the previous two forms of organizational forgetting, which by definition were accidental, both *unlearning* and *avoiding bad habits* are very conscious forms of ensuring unwanted knowledge is not embedded in organizational memories. Applied correctly, the active process of intentional forgetting will increase an organization's competitiveness (de Holan et al., 2004). So how is it that this counterintuitive idea may increase competitiveness?

The first of the intentional techniques is unlearning, which Holan et al. describe as "to unlearn knowledge, a company intentionally removes something that is well established in an organization's memory" (de Holan et al., 2004, p. 49). The something to which they refer may be a process or routine or even the divestment of a business unit. A good example of the former is the Permanent Joint Board on Defense. U.S. President Franklin D. Roosevelt and Canadian Prime Minister King established this high-level Canadian-American forum in 1941. In a joint press release, the two leaders announced the Ogdensburg Declaration, as shown in Figure 6.

The Ogdensburg Declaration (Maloney, 1997, p. 5)

The Prime Minister and the President have discussed the mutual problems of defense in relation to the safety of Canada and the United States.

In has been agreed that a Permanent Joint Board on Defense be set up at once by the two countries.

The permanent Joint Board on Defense shall commence immediate studies relating to sea, land, and air problems including personnel and material.

It will consider in the broad sense the defense of the north half of the Western hemisphere.

The Permanent Joint Board on Defense will consist of four or five members from each country, most of them from the services. It will meet shortly.

Figure 6. The Ogdensburg Declaration

Indeed, the group met for the first time 7 days later and has met over 200 times since. Almost certainly, the success of the group has been its ability to change over time but to remain true to the terse direction provided by President Roosevelt and Prime Minister King. Several times throughout its history, intentional forgetting was instrumental in achieving its mission.

In the early days of the Board, every word of every meeting was carefully transcribed into the minutes of the Board. This provided a rich *record* of the meeting; however, it was also somewhat artificial. Both the American and Canadian delegations were very conscious that stakeholders would also scrutinize this rich record for years to come. Indeed, the record became somewhat of a barometer of Canada–U.S. relations. When tensions existed between the two countries, the tension could be read in the Board minutes.

To avoid the appearance of disagreement, many contentious issues were removed from the agenda. These *politically correct* removals may have served the needs of some stakeholders; however, this led to many important binational issues being shelved. To ensure that real issues were not overlooked, unofficial meetings were commonplace. In these sidebars, top officials were free to have open and frank but unrecorded discussions. Officially, these talks never occurred, as they were not recorded in the detailed minutes.

Over time, this practice did not serve the Board well. For a variety of reasons, the Board leadership decided to *forget* the routine of capturing every word and moved to a system of recording only the decisions, not the detailed discussion that preceded the decision. For some, this decision was seen to destroy the verbose history that heretofore had been captured for generations to come. However, the reality was that the transcriptions were preventing the open and frank discussions that were necessary to ensure the best decisions were taken.

An equally important act of intentional forgetting took place immediately following the attacks of September 11. For more than a decade before this fateful day, the Board's power, both legitimate and referent, had been eroded. The fall of communism and the destruction of the Berlin Wall marked a new world order. Political leaders were quick to declare a *peace dividend,* which resulted in a shift of focus away from defense and security to one of economic development. For the Board this meant fewer important issues to consider.

The long-standing history, tradition, and reputation of the Board meant that neither country wished to dismantle it—But what to do? One solution was to make the Board more of an icon of the great relationship between the countries and to remind citizens of both countries of the great work the Board had accomplished when needed. The Board continued to meet and discuss issues of mutual interest; however, few serious or actionable recommendations were made in the 1990s.

As we all know, the world changed on September 11, 2001, and so did the Board. Instantly, there was renewed interest in the Board's mission, *to consider in the broad sense the defense of the north half of the Western hemisphere.* Just as President Roosevelt and Prime Minister King had imagined, there was a need for strong bilateral relations.

The Board's leadership realized that organizational forgetting would play an important part in achieving its stated mission. A decade of meetings had been largely symbolic and lacked substance, crisscrossing each country in a competition to see who could out-host the other. Clearly, the post-9/11 meetings would have to be different, and they were. The first official meeting was held in Ottawa on October 10, 2001. The tone was different as were the guest speakers; both the Canadian Chief of Defence Staff (Canada's most senior General) and the Canadian Defence Minister addressed this Board.

Once again, the meetings were all about substance and not pomp and circumstance. Once again, the meetings added real value, just as President Roosevelt and Prime Minister King would have wished. Once again, organizational forgetting was key to the longevity of the Board.

The second part of intentional forgetting is *avoiding bad habits.* Early in John's career, he witnessed the impact of exactly this phenomenon. The organization in which he was a young manager was renowned for doing things the same as they always had—to say they were creatures of habit is an understatement. The organization culture believed firmly that what was done in the past was always the correct course of action. In fact, this was so common that the acronym SALT, or *same as last time,* was often used to highlight that the idea under consideration had already been "solved." As fate would have it, a new leader arrived and insisted the organization avoid the bad habits associated with SALT. Initially, the transition was difficult, but later the organization accepted the revolutionary concept of trying new ideas.

We are critical of some organizations that apply the SALT technique, as we see this as an innovation killer. That said, there are certainly times that it makes incredible sense. We live in a very small city that hosts the largest Scandinavian festival in North America. For more than 40 years, the city of Minot, North Dakota, becomes the temporary home to visitors from around the world for one week in the fall. During Norsk Høstfest, an army of more than 7,000 volunteers transforms our city into a Scandinavian celebration. Over the years, the leadership team has refined this transformation to an amazing degree—virtually everything is SALT and virtually everybody is happy year after year.

Virtual Memories

Every now and then, we think we know things that we really do not know. Often this is the result of virtual memories, a term JoAnn coined to describe John's frequent and annoying lack of recall about important events in our lives. Rather than be upset that John could not remember their first dinner at a special little pub in London or café in Paris, JoAnn would ask him to have a virtual memory—allowing us both to enjoy the special moment. These virtual memories have become so common in our family that even our granddaughter Sara is often heard saying, "Well, Grandpa just has a virtual memory."

Occasionally, these virtual memories take over, and for reasons John cannot explain he seems more able to remember these virtual occurrences than the original events. We suspect that there is some psychological theory that would explain this bizarre phenomenon. In any case, we have witnessed others display the characteristics of virtual memories. Next time you are mingling at a cocktail party, riding the commuter train home, or watching a little league ball game, listen for these telltale words: "Oh yes, now I remember." This is almost certainly the early stages of virtual memories creation. Next comes, "wasn't there a _____ there?" or some other statement of the obvious. This in turn triggers the "yeah that's right," and now we have a virtual memory.

So here we are, certain that we said, heard, or did something. We suppose all in all that it is a pretty harmless state of affairs until we witness this play out in the boardroom. Virtual memories really have no place in a work environment. That is not to say they do not exist—au contraire—simply that they are best left to more risk-free venues such as home (did we really say that?).

Nancy Dixon, a first-class speaker on the subject of knowledge in organizations, has an excellent exercise that goes some way to prove our point. About halfway through her exciting chat on how knowledge may be used to create competitive advantage, she pauses and announces that it is audience participation time. Like clockwork, you can hear a groan of disbelief and murmuring such as "I hate these little exercises" or "I came to listen, not be part of the show." Fearlessly, she announces that there will be a test. This causes a hullabaloo and the audience becomes even more vocal. One or two suddenly have to powder their noses and run for cover. Another is seen answering a cell phone, which is turned off, and politely excuses himself to deal with an *office emergency*.

Those brave souls who remain are in for a treat. The next couple of minutes promise to be extremely interesting, the kind of stuff that creates lasting memories—no virtual recollections here. The rules are simple enough: all participants are to take a pen and a piece of paper. Nancy will say 10 words, after which each audience member is to try to write as many of the words as they remember. Once all 10 words are on our list, then we are to put our pen down, signaling our competition. We will have 5 minutes to complete the exercise. "Ready?" she says. The grunts, head nodding, and shoulder shrugging seem to indicate that we are ready as we will ever be and so it begins. She reads the following words, slowly, being very careful to enunciate each one:

Bed	Slumber
Rest	Night
Pajamas	Awake
Pillow	Blanket
Snore	Dream

Then comes the command *Go!* The audience is given exactly 5 minutes to write down the 10 words. Busy as beavers, people are furiously writing the words they can remember. After about one minute there is more scratching of heads then writing. A few people try to share answers, but the eagle-eyed Nancy reminds us, *this is an individual exercise and, in respect for others, we should be very quiet.* We obey. The clock seems to be ticking in slow motion. She announces, *you have 2 minutes left.* She encourages us to *recall all 10 words.* Next comes the one-minute warning. Many people are struggling as they only have nine words and they really want to remember the last one. *Thirty seconds* she says. Nothing, they still have only nine words. Fifteen seconds. All of sudden, they remember the 10th word and write it down. What a relief. *10-9-8-7-6-5-4-3-2-1, please put down your pens.*

Next, she asks for a show of hands, how many people have *seven or more words?* Most people put up their hands. *How about eight or more words?* A few hands drop but it is still pretty impressive. *Nine or more?* Hmmm, that is strange—most people still have their hands up. *Ten?* A few hands drop, but there are still more than many anticipated. She starts to move on to another subject, and there is public outcry—those who missed a word or two want to know which one(s) they missed.

This is when the real fun begins. She reads the words one by one and asks for a show of hands. Virtually everyone wrote down the first five words: bed, rest, pajamas, pillow, and snore. Next she says, "sleep." There is a sudden drop in hands; now only about half the audience raises their hand. They are very proud to be one of this special group. At this point, she asks everyone with *sleep* on their list to keep their hands up high as she counts us. As she is counting the hands, she puts up a PowerPoint slide with the 10 words.

The audience becomes alive with conversation. As it turns out the word *sleep* was not on the original list and yet more than 50% of us wrote down the word. She tells us this is normal; 50% of us added a word that she did not read. Clearly, people are surprised; however, we quickly real-ize this is a word-association issue. All of the words are related to sleep so, as we were struggling to recall words, our brains helped us out and added the word that should have been on the list.

The message behind this exercise is very telling. More than 50% of us added extra data to this message being sent. To us, this extra word was a fact. We could use the fact to create information and eventually knowledge. Of course, this is the problem with flawed data. The Chinese philosopher Confucius stated almost 2,500 years ago, "When you say something, say what you know, When you don't know something, say that you don't know. That is knowledge" (as quoted in Crainer, 1997).

Information Anxiety

So far in this chapter, we have considered the ideas of organizational forgetting and virtual memories. Both of these are rather intentional instruments that we choose to use or not. From a knowledge management perspective, both of these are deliberate processes where individuals or organizations choose to apply the knowledge they know. But what if knowledge existed in your organization, knowledge that you knew existed, but was unavailable to you?

The genesis of a recent project was the belief that the downsizing, rightsizing, or whatever the politically correct euphemism for events during the late 20th century created an environment in which many middle managers were having difficulty dealing with the increasing volume of information. In 2001, Dr. Nick Bontis of McMaster University eloquently reminded us that the total accumulated codified database of the world would double twice a day by 2010 (Bontis, 2001). He suggested that in 2010, people would awake daily knowing half of what we knew the day before. Even though he was joking, his point remains valid—information is growing at an exponential rate.

Some might argue that downsizing exercises of the 1990s are history and not of much interest today. We would argue the opposite. It seems very plausible that in the next few years we may witness similar, possibly hasted or poorly planned reorganizations in an attempt to deal with the global economic challenges ahead of us. We think there are many lessons to be learned from the 1990s, one of which surrounds information anxiety.

If Nick Bontis's revelations become reality or even partially true, then information overload must be one of the major menaces confronting middle managers in this new millennium. Some gurus suggest there is more to the information tribulations of the new era than simply overload. The term overload seems to imply that limiting the quantity of information will solve the problem. Increasingly, research indicates that there are other information challenges with even greater impact. The collective noun for this group of challenges is *information anxiety*.

Contrary to popular belief, information overload is not the issue that should concern executives. As it turns out, the middle managers are far more concerned about something else. They are concerned about a more debilitating aliment titled *accessing information.* In this case, accessing information has nothing to do with *access to information* legislation but rather with a component of *information anxiety* first described by Richard Wurman (1989) nearly two decades ago.

Earlier we suggested that, somehow, there was a link between the concepts of information overload (or the many other terms used to describe the malady) and the cognitive hierarchy. However, this required a temporary leap of faith, as there was little substance to support the claim. Having exposed the necessary theory of the cognitive hierarchy, let us return to this important link.

Neither information overload nor the study of the subject is new. According to David Bawden (2001), more than 245 academic papers were produced on the subject between 1972 and 2000. Predictably, despite the vast quantity of research, there is not a single, accepted definition for information overload. In fact, there is even debate about the best term to use. Many suggest information overload (Bawden, 2001; Speier et al., 1999), while others recommend terms such as information anxiety (Wurman, 1989) and cognitive overload (Kirsh, 2000). Despite the variety of labels and characterizations, there are a number of recurring themes.

Some researchers suggest, "Information Overload occurs when the amount of input to a system exceeds its processing capacity" (Speier et al., 1999, p. 338). This definition assumes that quantity alone is the concern and therefore does not consider if the quality of information is relevant to the problem. Bawden (2001) writes, "Information overload is that state in which available, and potentially useful, information is a hindrance rather than a help" (p. 6). Bawden widens the scope of the definition by suggesting that relevance may be an important factor.

Wilson (2001) adds value to the debate by including two additional factors. First, he divides the problem into two parts, a personal problem and an organizational problem. Second, he introduces the concept of perception to the definition. In other words, the decision if a problem exists or not lies with the effected person or organization. Wilson (2001) defines personal information overload as "a perception on the part of the individual (or observers of that person) that the flow of information associated with work tasks is greater than can be managed effectively" (p. 113). Wilson adds organizational information overload is "a situation in which the extent of perceived information overload is sufficiently widespread within an organization as to reduce the overall effectiveness of management operations" (p. 113).

Others broaden the scope even further by dealing with issues of infrastructure and the uncertainty surrounding the existence of a particular piece of information. For example, in his book *Information Anxiety*, Richard Wurman (1989) defines information anxiety as "the black hole between data and knowledge. It happens when information doesn't tell us what we want or need to know" (p. 34). Kirsh (2000) opted not to provide an actual definition; instead, he related four causes of cognitive overload, which are too much information supply, too much information demand, the need to deal with multitasking and interruption, and the inadequate workplace infrastructure to help reduce metacognition.

Wurman (1989) introduces a novel notion while describing information anxiety by stating, "Information anxiety can afflict us at any level and is as likely to result from too much information as too little information" (p. 44). This concept is fundamental to comprehend, as many researchers focus entirely on the idea of information overload and thus infer that the only challenge is too much information. Wurman notes that a major cause of information anxiety is the uncertainty surrounding the existence of a particular piece of information.

Based on recent knowledge management studies, these wider characterizations appear more appropriate. For example, the authors of Gartner Research's Information Overload Survey concluded there are four information issues affecting competition: siloed information, too much information, unindexed information, and ineffective searching procedures (Linden et al., 2002). In a second report, Linden suggests there are seven drivers of information overload: quantity, relevance, redundancy, information illiteracy, unqualified information, distraction by the obvious and the glossy, and business models struggling (Linden, 2001).

The consideration of the wider classification of this information challenge is more pertinent than one focused solely on some of the narrow definitions provided. The latter implies a technological solution to reduce the quantity of information, perhaps by eliminating duplicate data. This may ease the size of the problem and may well be a part of the ultimate solution; however, the challenge is more complex and not merely an issue of quantity. Research underscores other associated concerns, which from a management point of view are equally important. For example, simply reducing the quantity of information will do nothing to assist in Wurman and Kirsh's concerns of not knowing where to find information. The five components of information anxiety are

1. not understanding information;
2. feeling overwhelmed by the amount of information to be understood;
3. not knowing if certain information exists;
4. not knowing where to find information; and
5. knowing exactly where to find the information, but not having the key to access it (Wurman, 1989, p. 44).

As it turns out, middle managers reported accessing information, Wurman's latter category, as the most troubling component of information anxiety. Middle managers reported levels for this component were statistically higher than either understanding information or information overload. Of course, some cases of this problem are simply unfortunate oversights; perhaps a manager knows that a document exists, but it is in a locked filing cabinet and neither the key nor the combination is available. Organizationally, this is quite minor because we can always change polices to ensure managers have access (Girard, 2005a).

But, what if the barriers are deliberate? Deliberate barriers, which do exist, are far more serious and much more difficult to change. This is what keeps managers awake at night. In fact, this is a management failure of the highest magnitude and should serve as a clear wake-up call to organizational leaders. Middle managers must have immediate and unobstructed access to the information they require to perform their tasks. The dismantling of these pointless barricades to accessing this goldmine of information is within the gift of management. There are few, if any, technological, legal, or organizational reasons to sanction these obstacles.

Regrettably, anecdotal evidence suggests the root of these obstacles is an environment of mistrust. If senior executives would only trust their middle managers, who are the custodians of this organizational treasure, to access the information they deem necessary, the problem would undoubtedly vanish. Even though a stroke of a pen would solve this issue, there seems to be continued reluctance on the part of executives to do so.

Although accessing information was reported by middle managers as the most important issue, two others are worthy of note. Two other information challenges were rated as at least as significant. The first is *information exists* (defined as *not knowing* if information exists) and the second is *finding information* (defined as *not knowing* where to find information). Executives should pay attention to these troubling findings. They should acknowledge the breadth and depth of the problem and then develop a strategy to improve the situation.

These three concerns share a common origin—the need for middle managers to have access to information they need to perform their tasks. Firstly, they cannot access what they need to know. Secondly, the managers do not know if information exists. Thirdly, they do not know where to find the information. This is the essence of knowledge management—ensuring that those who have the need to know do in fact know what they need to know and where to get it.

Remember Richard Wurman

Two decades ago, Richard Wurman released the best-selling book *Information Anxiety*. The fascinating book explored a variety of interesting and thought-provoking ideas, many of which captured the attention of managers suffering from information bombardment. Of particular interest to us was Wurman's notion that *information anxiety* was the black hole between data and knowledge, claiming it happens when information does not tell us what we want or need to know.

Now You Know . . .

- There are four modes of organizational forgetting: *Memory decay and failure to capture* are the accidental modes of organizational memory loss. *Unlearning and avoiding bad habits* are the intentional modes of organizational memory loss.
- **Information Overload** occurs when the amount of input to a system exceeds its processing capacity (Speier et al., 1999,

p. 338). Alternatively, information overload is described as that state in which available, and potentially useful, information is a hindrance rather than a help (Bawden, 2001, p. 6).

- **Information Anxiety** is the black hole between data and knowledge. It happens when information does not tell us what we want or need to know. The five components of information anxiety are not understanding information; feeling overwhelmed by the amount of information to be understood; not knowing if certain information exists; not knowing where to find information; and knowing exactly where to find the information, but not having the key to access it (Wurman, 1989, p. 44).

- **Organizational Information Overload** is a situation in which the extent of perceived information overload is sufficiently widespread within an organization as to reduce the overall effectiveness of management operations (Wilson, 2001, p. 113).

- **Personal Information Overload** is a perception on the part of the individual (or observers of that person) that the flow of information associated with work tasks is greater than can be managed effectively (Wilson, 2001, p. 113).

CHAPTER 6

Tools, Tactics, and Techniques: Tried and Tested

I wish we knew what we know at HP.

—Lew Platt, Hewlett-Packard (O'Dell et al., 1998)

Now that we have deduced that there are some things that we want to know and others that we want to forgot, the question becomes how, as an organization, can we know what we want to know? The focus is now on how today's successful leaders are using knowledge management to create an enterprise advantage. The vehicle for this exploration is Michael Earl's 5-year research project, in which he proposes a taxonomy of the strategies, or schools, for knowledge management (Earl, 2001). Earl's self-confessed purpose was to help guide executives on choices to initiate knowledge management projects according to the goals, organizational charter, and technological, behavioral, or economic biases. In categorizing the schools, Earl used three biases (technological, behavioral, and economic) as the high-order categories. Further dissecting these categories results in seven unique schools (Earl, 2001).

Earl's work is not the only project to categorize the types or domains of knowledge management; however, we consider it one of the most useful for leaders. The depth of Earl's research, combined with the practical nature of his recommendations, makes Earl's work a particularly useful guide for leaders. Another high quality project comes from Xerox researchers at their Palo Alto Research Center (PARC) who established their own categories (Xerox, 2001b). Together, these two works provide an excellent conduit to explore the spectrum of knowledge management categorization. What follows is an overview of Earl's seven schools along with examples of real-world implementations highlighting the major advantages of the school. The Xerox findings, as well as those of others, supplement Earl's thesis by means of reinforcing his conclusions.

To some degree, you may consider this chapter the *State of Knowledge Management* circa 2000. We will highlight tools, tactics, and techniques that leaders successfully implemented in the past decade. Most of the ideas are mature and have proven to be successful. In the next chapter, we will explore some new ideas that have not yet passed the test of time, but for now, let us focus on what we know works.

The System School

Earl classifies his first group, *technocratic*, as each of the schools relies on information technology to assist *knowledge workers*. The term knowledge worker was first coined in 1959 by the esteemed management guru Peter Drucker. Many authors have used the term, often with quite different meanings. For our purposes, we will use Tom Davenport's description from *Thinking for a Living*, in which he wrote, "Knowledge workers have high degrees of expertise, education, or experience, and the primary purpose of their jobs involves the creation, distribution, or application of knowledge" (Davenport, 2005, p. 10).

Earl suggests information technology could provide knowledge bases, knowledge directories, or knowledge flows in the three Technocratic schools: systems, cartographic, and engineering.

The purpose of the system school is "to capture specialist knowledge in knowledge bases which other specialist or qualified people can access" (Earl, 2001, p. 218). For many, this is the essence of knowledge management, the ability to access knowledge quickly to help solve an

	Technocratic School (Earl, 2001)		
School Attribute	**System**	**Cartographic**	**Engineering**
Focus	Technology	Maps	Processes
Aim	Knowledge bases	Knowledge directories	Knowledge flows
Philosophy	Codification	Connectivity	Capability

Figure 7. Earl's Technocratic School

organizational challenge. An example would be reducing the time middle managers spend searching for knowledge or information. A successful implementation of the system school may reduce or eliminate the challenges postulated by Wurman (1989), who noted that a major cause of information anxiety is the uncertainty surrounding the existence of a particular piece of information.

One of the best examples of the systems school is Xerox's best knowledge-sharing practice, code-named Eureka. Eureka helps Xerox field technicians to quickly and accurately diagnose, solve, and prevent equipment problems. Eureka contains a vast database of knowledge derived from the more than one million annual service calls completed by Xerox's customer service engineers. Eureka seeks to complement the explicit knowledge contained in standard service manuals with the tacit knowledge engineers amass through experience.

Developed jointly by technicians in Xerox France and scientists at Xerox PARC, Eureka epitomizes collaboration. Together they codified the technicians' solutions to very difficult, complex, and rare problems that tended to be learned from experience and passed from one technician to another through war stories (Xerox, 2001a). By 2002, more than 25,000 engineers in 71 countries were equipped with Eureka allowing them to service quickly customers' equipment, thereby reducing downtime and improving customer satisfaction. Although the concept sounds incredibly simple, the reality is that Eureka has saved the company more than $15 million while solving more than 350,000 service problems in a single year (Roberts-Witt, 2002).

A more recent and less known example of the system school in action is Intel's Expertise Location System, or ELS. The domain of expertise location offers incredible potential for large organizations to begin *knowing what they know* by facilitating the finding of organization knowledge. An American Productivity and Quality Center consortium learning forum report suggested, "As organizations become more complex and more globally dispersed, and as expertise becomes more specialized, leaders are looking for methods to help employees determine where to search and find answers" (O'Dell, 2003, p. 6).

The Intel system provides knowledge seekers the ability to query the expertise location system for solutions to business problems. If an answer is not discovered in the codified knowledge base, the question is routed to an expert, which may be an individual or a group of experts. According to the APQC ELS report, "Once an expert answers the question, the system automatically captures and stores [codifies] the solution. In some instances, the system may push the solution out to a subscriber-base interested in the particular area of discussion" (O'Dell, 2003, p. 8).

Key to the success of these systems is the input from experts. David Snowden, a thought leader in the sphere of knowledge management, articulated a third-generation model for knowledge management. Included in this new model are three heuristics, the first of which is "knowledge can only be volunteered; it cannot be conscripted" (Snowden, 2002, p. 102). This premise is why the Intel ELS and Eureka systems work so well. The experts volunteer the knowledge they are inputting to the systems, and by doing so they feel like an important part of the organization.

The Cartographic School

The second category, the cartographic school, is not surprisingly based on mapping organizational knowledge. The purpose of this school is "to make sure knowledgeable people in the organization are accessible to others for advice, consultation, or knowledge exchange" (Earl, 2001, p. 220). Finding the person who holds the particular knowledge is the key to this school. Perhaps the best analogy for this school is the yellow pages, as its main aim is the establishment of a knowledge directory that allows people to connect. Xerox describes this concept as mapping knowledge of experts "so people can locate and access knowledge or expertise held by certain people in an organization" (Xerox, 2001b). The cartographic school would likely diminish the negative effects of ineffective searching procedures postulated by a Gartner researcher in a paper titled *Information Not Yet at Your Fingertips? Here's Why* (Linden, 2001).

Snowden suggests, "Expertise location systems replace the second-generation technique of yellow pages making connections between people and communities" (Snowden, 2002, p. 109). A pioneering example of a modified yellow page implementation of the cartographic school is Lotus's ExpertLink (Lotus, 2001a). Rather than simply providing an automated version of the corporate directory that may result in frustrated knowledge seekers who are unable to locate the needed knowledge, the Lotus system was designed to ensure the most appropriate expert responds to customer queries. ExpertLink constantly monitored a number of internal systems including Lotus's workflow management system, Lotus's online employee question-and-answer forum, and Lotus's organizational directory. By monitoring this information, ExpertLink maintained a dynamic directory of experts. Upon receipt of a customer's query, ExpertLink quickly and automatically routes the inquiry to the most qualified product specialist. A real benefit of this system over more traditional directories is the dynamic nature of the expert selection as these experts may change over time.

The basis of this school complements Snowden's second heuristic of the new knowledge management generation, which is "we can always know more than we can tell, and we will always tell more than we can write down" (Snowden, 2002, p. 102). In ExpertLink-type systems, it is vital that the *expert* be found to deal with customers as the expert knows more than they are able to codify. In other words, relying solely on previously codified knowledge may only paint part of the picture.

The Engineering School

The last in technocratic taxonomy is the engineering school, which focuses on two related concepts. The first is that "performance of business processes can be enhanced by providing operating personnel with knowledge relevant to their task" and second that "management processes are inherently more knowledge-intensive than business processes" (Earl, 2001, p. 221).

An example that combines Earl's thesis with Xerox's ideas is Novartis's Consumer Health's knowledge management system designed to expedite the U.S. Food and Drug Administration's (FDA) submission process. Their DocuKnowledge Suite not only supports the quick creation and tendering of FDA submissions but also eliminates unnecessary repetition of the mistakes based on the experience from previous submissions. The system ensures that all submission documents are included and in the correct format, thereby reducing unnecessary delays searching for lost paper documents. The result is a best practice solution that ensures products get to market quicker and therefore capture greater sales opportunities. The basis of the system is simple, ensuring employees know what they must do (in this case, FDA submission guidelines) and to ensure they do not repeat mistakes (best practices; Lotus, 2001b).

Earl argues that in addition to decision-related information, best practice knowledge is also very important. Xerox (2001b) terms this concept *capturing and reusing past experiences* highlighting that companies should seek to capture and organize knowledge for reuse in subsequent projects.

The Commercial School

A single school exists within the *economic* category that is titled the commercial school. Earl defines this school as economic because "it is overtly and explicitly concerned with both protecting and exploiting a firm's knowledge or intellectual assets to produce revenue streams" (Earl, 2001, p. 222). Xerox (2001b) suggests that companies should understand and measure the value of knowledge and be able to leverage intellectual assets.

	Economic School (Earl, 2001)
School Attribute	**Commercial**
Focus	Income
Aim	Knowledge assets
Philosophy	Commercialization

Figure 8. Earl's Economic School

An acknowledged leader in this field is Dow Chemicals. In the 1990s, Dow established teams to review the value of their patents and discovered that 25% of their patents had no business value. In a 2001 speech, Dow Vice President Richard Gross (2001) stated Dow was able to reduce their patent holdings by over 10,000, resulting in a savings of $40 million in 5 years. In addition, Dow was able to donate a number of patents thereby achieving a substantial tax credit. By developing tools and processes, Gross (2001) stated Dow was able to extract more value and generate more revenue from intangible assets.

The Organizational School

The last group of Earl's schools is the behavioral group, which stems from the social sciences and focuses on the creation, sharing, and use of knowledge as a resource. Concentrating on collaboration, contactivity, and consciousness, many consider this group to be the people group, once again emphasizing the notion that technology is not the exclusive foundation of knowledge management (Earl, 2001).

Earl describes the organizational school as "the use of organizational structures, or networks to share or pool knowledge" (Earl, 2001, p. 223). Xerox simply describes this domain as *knowledge sharing* (Xerox, 2001b). Xerox research indicates that 42% of organizational knowledge is in the minds of workers, and only 12% of corporate knowledge is in a knowledge base available for sharing within the organization (Xerox, 2001c). Clearly, the key to success of this school is maximizing the amount of knowledge sharing and thereby reducing the time wasted seeking knowledge.

An interesting example of this school is the cross-reference, or Xref, system used by Northrop Grumman. Facing the drawdown of the B-2 project, the company decided it would be necessary to "maintain profiles of staff who could be used for future B-2 projects" (O'Dell, 2003, p. 13). The Xref system is managed by Northrop Grumman's knowledge management team, which "is chartered to enable the reuse of 'what we know,' regardless of location . . . and collaboration across boundaries" (O'Dell, 2003, p. 13). Earl suggests, "An important feature of knowledge communities is that they bring together knowledge and knowers" (Earl, 2001, p. 223). This key element of the organizational school, which is connecting knowledge seekers with knowledge providers through knowledge pooling and collaboration,

School Attribute	Behavioral School (Earl, 2001)		
	Organizational	Spatial	Strategic
Focus	Networks	Space	Mindset
Aim	Knowledge pooling	Knowledge exchange	Knowledge capabilities
Philosophy	Collaboration	Contactivity	Consciousness

Figure 9. Earl's Behavioral School

was the dominate model of the APQC Expertise Location Study (O'Dell, 2003).

By far our favorite example of organizational knowledge management is communities of practice. Earl suggests, "An important feature of knowledge communities is that they bring together knowledge and knowers" (Earl, 2001, p. 223). In their book *Leveraging Communities of Practice for Strategic Advantage*, authors Hubert Saint-Onge and Debra Wallace describe a community of practice as "a place where people generate new knowledge that increases stocks and facilitates the flow of knowledge capital in an organization" (Saint-Onge & Wallace, 2003, p. 27). We like to think of communities of practices as groups of passionate volunteers who embrace the need to share principle.

The Spatial School

The spatial school provides "a design for emergence philosophy of knowledge management . . . it centers on the use of space or spatial designs to facilitate knowledge exchange" (Earl, 2001, p. 225). Many scholars refer to this school using a watercooler metaphor—as workers gather at the watercooler to exchange information and knowledge. In *Working Knowledge*, Davenport and Prusak (1998) argue convincingly that conversations around the watercooler provide an opportunity for knowledge transfer (presumably tacit knowledge).

Davenport and Prusak warn us of modern management practices that consider socializing wasteful or purport virtual offices as the way of the future. Alan Webber supports this thesis and believes, "In the new economy, conversations are the most important form of work. Conversations are the way knowledge workers discover what they know, share it with their colleagues, and in the process create new knowledge" (Webber, 1993, p. 28). This school builds on the foundation of Snowden's final heuristic, which is "we only know what we know when we need to know it" (Snowden, 2002, p. 102). Simply put, unless or until we understand the context of a question, we are often unable to answer the question or share our knowledge.

An excellent and time-proven example of the spatial school comes from the British army, where it has long been a tradition for all officers of a regiment to meet for coffee in the morning. Like clockwork, the officers meet at 10 o'clock every day. To outsiders, this may simply appear to be another case of the British class system in action; however, nothing could be further from the truth. In fact, this daily meeting allows officers to discuss current challenges and seek the advice and counsel of those more experienced. In days gone by, the officers may have discussed the best way to ride or shoe a particular mare. Today, they may be discussing the complex issue of detainees of the war on terrorism. The discussions tend to revolve around difficult situations, the solutions to which remain uncodified within army manuals. This informal exchange of knowledge is a classic transfer of tacit knowledge, a transfer of knowledge that would not transpire if the meeting did not take place in such an informal manner.

A final example of this school is the Japanese concept of *ba*, which, according Ikujiro Nonaka and Noboru Konno,

> can be thought of as a shared space for emerging relationships. This space can be physical (e.g., office, dispersed business space), virtual (e.g., e-mail, teleconference), mental (e.g., shared experiences, ideas, ideals), or any combination of them. What differentiates *ba* from ordinary human interaction is the concept of knowledge creation. *Ba* provides a platform for advancing individual and/or collective knowledge. It is from such a platform that a transcendental perspective integrates all information needed. (Nonaka & Konno, 1998, p. 40)

A number of U.S. organizations have tried to adopt the *ba* concept, with varied results. One ambitious young executive is rumored to have caught the attention of the Board when he suggested their corporate headquarters should have a *ba* with an R or *bar*—we do not think that is quite what the doctor ordered.

The Strategic School

The strategic school "sees knowledge management as a dimension of competitive strategy" (Earl, 2001, p. 227). This school seeks to exploit knowledge itself as a resource. Those practicing the strategic school consider knowledge, on its own, to be a strategic advantage. Earl cites examples of companies, which harvest knowledge as a resource. However, this school should be considered a follow-up or mature strategy as few organizations would be able to plan on knowledge becoming its major asset. It seems much more likely that successful knowledge management organizations will use this school once they have achieved success following one of the other schools.

A renowned case of the organizational knowledge management school metamorphosing into a strategic school is Buckman Laboratories. Recall from an earlier chapter that Buckman Laboratories is a chemical manufacturer and distributor headquartered in Memphis, Tennessee. They sell more than 1,000 different specialist chemical products around the world while employing over 1,200 people. However, recently they have become more renowned for their innovative corporate knowledge management network. Today, business leaders from some of the highest technology sectors visit Buckman Laboratories to learn about knowledge management.

Remember Michael Earl

Michael Earl (2001) is the author of a research report that proposes a taxonomy of the strategies, or schools, for knowledge management. Earl's self-confessed purpose in developing the 5-year study was to help guide executives on choices to initiate knowledge management projects according to the goals, organizational charter, and technological, behavioral, or economic biases. In categorizing the schools, Earl used three biases (technological, behavioral, and economic) as the high-order categories. Dissecting these categories further results in seven unique schools.

Now You Know . . .

- The purpose of the **Cartographic School** is to make sure knowledgeable people in the organization are accessible to others for advice, consultation, or knowledge exchange (Earl, 2001, p. 220).

- The **Commercial School** is overtly and explicitly concerned with both protecting and exploiting a firm's knowledge or intellectual assets to produce revenue streams (Earl, 2001, p. 222).
- The **Engineering School** focuses on two related concepts. The first is that performance of business processes can be enhanced by providing operating personnel with knowledge relevant to their task and second that management processes are inherently more knowledge-intensive than business processes (Earl, 2001, p. 221).
- The focus of the **Organizational School** is on the use of organizational structures, or networks to share or pool knowledge (Earl, 2001, p. 223).
- The **Spatial School** provides a design for emergence philosophy of knowledge management. It centers on the use of space or spatial designs to facilitate knowledge exchange (Earl, 2001, p. 225).
- The **Strategic School** sees knowledge management as a dimension of competitive strategy (Earl, 2001, p. 227).
- The aim of the **System School** is to capture specialist knowledge in knowledge bases, which other specialist or qualified people can access (Earl, 2001, p. 218).

PART 3

Enhancing Future Performance

CHAPTER 7

Guiding Organizations Into the Future

Well that didn't actually happen, but . . . it could have!

—Geena Davis, *Actor and Raconteur*

In the past 5 years or so, there has been tremendous interest in the value of oral narrative or storytelling as a catalyst for organizational change. Many of these accounts chronicle seasoned executives telling *stories* that spark massive transformation in their organizations. It seems, so the story goes, that these organizations were apparently reluctant or incapable of considering even the most modest change initiative—that is, until the story was told. With that in mind, we thought a chapter on crafting future-based stories would be a fitting way to commence a glimpse of the future. Consider our interpretation of the classic *Cathedral Builder* story:

On a foggy autumn day, nearly 800 years ago, a traveler happened upon a large group of workers adjacent to the River Avon. Despite being tardy for an important rendezvous, curiosity convinced the traveler that he should inquire about their work. With a slight detour he moved toward the first of the three tradesmen and said, "My dear fellow what is it that you are doing?" The man continued his work and grumbled, "I am cutting stones." Realizing that the mason did not wish to engage in a conversation, the traveler moved toward the second of the three and repeated the question. To the traveler's delight, this time the man stopped his work, ever so briefly, and stated that he was a stonecutter. He then added, "I came to Salisbury from the north to work but as soon as I earn ten quid I will return home." The traveler thanked the second mason, wished him a safe journey home, and began to head to the third of the trio.

When he reached the third worker, he once again asked the original question. This time the worker paused, glanced at the traveler until they made eye contact, and then looked skyward drawing the traveler's eyes upward. The third mason replied, "I am a mason and I am building a cathedral." He continued, "I have journeyed many miles to be part of the team that is constructing this magnificent cathedral. I have spent many months away from my family and I miss them dearly. However, I know how important Salisbury Cathedral will be one day and I know how many people will find sanctuary and solace here. I know this because the Bishop once told me his vision for this great place. He described how people would come from all parts to worship here. He also told me that the Cathedral will not be completed in our days but that the future depends on our hard work." He paused and then said, "So I am prepared to be away from my family because I know it is the right thing to do. I hope that one day my son will continue in my footsteps and perhaps even his son if need be."

This story is an adaptation of a legendary example of how a well-told story can motivate men and women to make great sacrifices if they believe their work is important. One can imagine that most leaders would wish to have a team of cathedral builders rather than stonecutters. The question is, Can a story really transform stonecutters into cathedral builders?

To date, most of the work in the domain has focused on the value of telling stories—in other words, oral narrative. Take, for example, Steve Denning's book *The Springboard*, the subtitle of which is *How Storytelling Ignites Action in Knowledge-Era Organizations* (2001). In this seminal work, Denning describes his successes in telling face-to-face stories. Denning's work has spawned a host of other papers and books, most of which focus on telling oral stories.

Surely these printed exposés are themselves motivators for change; so why the continued emphasis on the face-to-face storytelling? Perhaps there is value in examining writing stories rather than telling stories that spark change. This chapter is a story of exactly that, writing stories that help guide organizations. We thought this would be a fitting topic to conclude our discussion of what leaders can do to guard the knowledge of their organizations. We believe that well-written stories are an excellent way to guide organizations into the future.

Getting the Message Right

> Stories are a primary mode of human communication and thinking—and one that has been used since the dawn of time. Why? Stories have depth and multiple dimensions; they help us create human connections in a world that seems complex, sometimes (or often) threatening, and increasingly dehumanizing. Stories give us context. ("Stories & Storytelling," 2005)

Before describing the stories, it is worth reviewing the literature with a view to determining the theoretical foundations of these stories. Much like the cathedral builder's bishop, many leaders use stories to electrify their subordinates and lead them into the future. The ability to relate to an audience using a story is a concept that has passed the test of time. Through a variety of approaches, present-day executives use stories to excite and invigorate their teams much as their predecessors did. Kaye and Jocobson remind us that "stories tap into our emotions and intellect in ways that get us to remember and use the information and wisdom of the past to help us make informed decisions in the future" (1999, p. 50).

There is an enormous difference between relating a message to an audience and sharing a vision to alter the future of an organization. The use of narration or storytelling envisage within a corporation can grant insight into an alternate course of action. Chartier, LaPointe, and Bonner state, in Get Real—*The Art and Power of Storytelling in Workplace Communities*, "Stories are a way to honour our past, describe our present and shape our future" (2005, p. v). The impact of conveying an envisioned story, which can change the future of an organization, can be magnificent, in the sense that it can also change lives. Yet, how does one know that the envisaged narrative will be received and have the ability to alter the future of an organization? How does the manager know if the message of their narrative has been received and that their team members can relate? In oral stories, the receivers demonstrate an attentive and responsive reaction, sometimes signs of enthusiasm. However, with the written word, the immediate reaction is often lacking.

Throughout time, leaders have used stories to share knowledge, spark change, and generally enlighten an audience. In a *Harvard Business Review* article titled "Telling Tales," Denning (2004) provides a catalog of seven types of stories used by leaders, including sparking action, communicating who you are, transmitting values, fostering collaboration, taming the grapevine, sharing knowledge, and leading people into the future.

Some leaders use formal presentations to achieve these tasks. Although there are similarities in the techniques, there are also significant differences. More and more, the evidence is suggesting the PowerPoint style of knowledge transfer is less effective than many believe. Janis Forman argues that "clear communications between executives and their audiences has been declining ever since the advent of souped-up computer graphics and Internet access to vast quantities of data" (1999, p. 1). Neilson and Stouffer (2005) claim that PowerPoint presentations lack contextual meaning. According to McKee and Fryer, we should "forget about PowerPoint and statistics. To involve people at the deepest level, you need stories" (2003, p. 51).

Steve Denning, the celebrated guru of storytelling, claims to have moved from PowerPoint-style presentations to storytelling after observing that his audience "merely looked dazed" (2004, p. 150). Larry Prusak, respected knowledge management expert, goes one step further by suggesting, "I've taken PowerPoint off all my computers; it's the enemy of thought" (Bell, 2004). Though Prusak's action may seem extreme, his point is very valid; knowledge sharing is sometimes impeded by an endless stream of charts and graphs.

In their article "Narrating the Vision," Neilson and Stouffer illustrate the effectiveness of using futuristic scenarios as a storytelling technique. They suggest that "futuristic scenarios—stories that paint a vivid picture of a future state—can help provide a vision and leadership in a narrative format as well as communicate the organization vision" (Neilson & Stouffer, 2005, p. 26). The ability to convey a message, as in the article "Narrating the Vision," is a great example of a futuristic scenario. Nevertheless, it is important to examine the effectiveness of the approach of futuristic scenarios within an organization. Steve Denning (2005) stated recently that future scenarios aid in the exploration of other points of view yet concluded that a descriptive narrative to support the scenario is necessary.

Conveying Futuristic Views

> As humans, we are wired to respond to stories in deep, sometimes unconscious ways. We actually answer with our attention and focus, when all other efforts may fail. Watch sometime how body language changes when someone starts a joke or story. Notice the slight rise in alertness and increased presence of the listeners. People will almost always put down what they are doing and give full attention. If the teller is particularly good at storytelling, then the response is almost always deep focus. (Baum, 2000, p. 159)

Visualizing a future organizational course of action entails strategies and tactics to build loyalty, focus effort, and spark creativity (Mai & Akerson, 2003). The *Leader as Communicator* exemplifies the restructuring of several organizations, each of which use stories to communicate a holistic viewpoint with one or more different angles. The basis of the story is a problematic statement posing a challenge for the organizations. The story is used to convey a guided future course of action for the organization; a methodical approach occurs prior to this phase. Before the plot line can be portrayed, a data-gathering process is needed. The data-gathering phase will answer questions on the past, current, and future courses of action of the organization. One should also consider the buy-in factor of stakeholders.

According to Forman (1999), one method that can be used to evaluate or test their envisaged narrative is an *analysis tree*. Determining coherence through a visual analysis illustrates phases within a story. The corporation's past history, current course of action to take, and the envisaged future will be shown along with the structural ideas that show a link to strategic reality. The analysis tree is similar to a storyboard, which allows visualization of how the process relates to another phase. This particular method was used by executives in the healthcare industry. The advantage of the analysis tree is flexibility to adapt to the storyteller's needs. The storyteller can adapt the analysis tree to the audience or stakeholders. Evaluating narratives through the analysis tree is valuable to an organization based on the effectiveness of the story.

Contrary to Forman's analysis tree, Allen (2005) suggests that storytelling will not substitute for analytical thinking, but only enhances organizational knowledge. However, sharing of knowledge ignites change, which increases the possibility of success within an organization. Altering duty into passion is a requirement to increase the level of accomplishments. Linking responsibilities with passions prevents burnout and remoteness among employees and therefore benefits the organization. Storytelling provides the means to convey messages to an audience or a method for sharing knowledge. "Storytelling can be the catalyst for change. . . . Telling your story complements analytical thinking and allows customers to engage feelings, leading to loyalty" (Allen, 2005, p. 64).

Storytelling can be advantageous to an organization in a variety of ways. "Stories can be told in a variety of modes that include: visual accounts, ballads, metaphors, text, and voice. Telling good stories serves the organization with an effective means of collecting wisdom through experience" (Matsui, n.d., p. 7). The use of storytelling, along with five other components, becomes useful for an organization to plan a future course of action. This form of planning is called *action mapping* and consists of assemblage, accumulation, and production of wisdom, actions as hypothesis, conservation of energy, reflection on action, as well as storytelling. The planning phase will consist of essential components from the data-gathering phase. Creating the story requires past, present, and future knowledge of the organization, which will in turn be used to develop the future course of action. Involving the stakeholders in the process creates an increased success factor of the envisaged narrative. Matsui suggests, "The knowledge and experiences gained from a journey clarify future actions by identifying emerging patterns."

Steve Denning (2001) uses the catalyst approach and takes storytelling a step further, through *springboard* stories, which provide the audience or stakeholders with a deeper level of understanding. Visualizing through the use of realistic events sustains the attention and consciousness of the audience. The significant aspect of a springboard story is the use of a simplistic approach, using fewer details to allow the audience to imagine the future possibilities that can occur within the organization. This catalyst approach leads the audience without controlling their views based on an individual's field or past experiences. Audience participation in the creation of the organization's future is met with less resistance and more enthusiasm, therefore obtaining buy-in from the participants.

Writing the Future

Snowden's second heuristic of the new knowledge management generation is that "we can always know more than we can tell, and we will always tell more than we can write down" (2002, p. 3). These wise words seem to suggest that telling an oral story may be more effective than a written story. However, before dismissing the written word, it is worth considering the context of his message. Snowden suggests,

> I can speak in five minutes what it will otherwise take me two weeks to get round to spending a couple of hours writing it down. The process of writing something down is reflective knowledge; it involves both adding and taking away from the actual experience or original thought. Reflective knowledge has high value, but is time consuming and involves loss of control over its subsequent use. (Snowden, 2002, p. 3)

This deeper examination of Snowden's second heuristic seems to imply that once one takes the time to create a written story, the value may be higher than a less reflective oral story. Snowden's premise is corroborated by Denning, who wrote, "A story can help take listeners, from where they are to where they need to be, by making them comfortable with an image of the future. The problem, of course, lies in crafting a credible narrative about the future when the future is unknowable" (2004, p. 127). Together, Denning and Snowden highlight the challenge of writing future stories—one must take the time to learn about the future and then articulate the ideas using the reflective knowledge Snowden described.

The overview concludes that, in theory, narratives help guide people into the future and share knowledge. The question remains, Can one use this technique in practice? Perhaps more specifically, the question is, Can one use written narratives to share knowledge and guide people into the future? One way to answer this question is by chronicling the success of three recently written stories. Each was written with the express aim of guiding people into the future.

Before describing the stories, it is important to understand that this chapter is based on our experiences and not based on empirical research nor does it report the results of a true experiment, but rather it describes the use of narratives in real organizations with real people dealing with real challenges. Most of the results are anecdotal in nature; nevertheless, it is believed that stories are a useful tool in some organizations.

There is no disputing the fact that oral narrative is a powerful form of communicating; however, it is not always feasible. In fact, there are times when the written word packs a more powerful punch. Often it is simply not possible to catch the ear of a wide audience simultaneously, or even at all. Many people simply will not take time from their busy schedules to listen to stories, others may be geographically separated, and still others may simply be *out to lunch* or otherwise predisposed. In these cases, the power of the pen offers a persuasive substitute.

This is a tale about a trio of such stories, which seemed to sow the seed of change, help guide people into the future, and share organizational knowledge. Of course, time will be the real test; however, anecdotal evidence seems to support the proposition that well-written futuristic stories provide an excellent alternative to face-to-face oral narrative. At least in these examples, the written story proved to be a motivator for organizational change and an effective way to share knowledge.

Story One—Guiding Government Leaders Into the Future

The first story was developed to excite change in a very large bureaucratic organization—Canada's Department of National Defence. At the time, John was leading the Strategic Knowledge Management cell and he was keen to explain how and why knowledge management could help Defence leaders. Clearly it would not be possible to meet face-to-face with all of the target audience, so what to do? Against the advice of many colleagues, pen was put to paper to create a story titled *Twelve Hours of Knowledge* (see Appendix 1). The story was an overwhelming success, and it was eventually included in the *Canadian Military Journal*—the journal read by the target audience (Girard, 2004a).

The story, which was set 5 years in the future, intentionally blurred the real with the imaginary. Many facets of the story were commonplace in Defence, such as the type of equipment, ranks, organizations, and jargon. Care was taken not to use any real people's names; instead, position titles were used. The tale was about a Canadian Forces operation on a small Caribbean island nation that was dealing with the aftermath of a natural disaster.

So what made the story a success? Clearly, there were a number of critical success factors; however, one of the most important was the *look* of the story. The story was designed to resemble the weekly newspaper of the Canadian Forces titled *The Maple Leaf.* With the editor's permission, a story was crafted that appeared to be *The Maple Leaf's* cover story. This allowed the story to be distributed as a *reprint* from the paper. The *look* was especially useful in capturing people's attention, countering to some degree the old cliché, "Don't judge a book by its cover." At least in this case it seems the *cover* was important to many people. Attracting the target audience is just the first step; clearly, the content is the vital ingredient.

Although the story was set in the future, it did not rely on futuristic technology, but rather, it described technology that is commonplace today. This was a surprise to many readers as they expected some far-fetched, ridiculously expensive *Star Trek*–type technology. Instead, the narrative described leadership and culture as the keys to success—another surprise to many readers.

A crucial component of the story's success was executive support. An early draft of the story caught the attention of one very senior executive who was delighted with the format and the message. His endorsement provided the necessary influence to sway a few less enthusiastic managers, who may have otherwise been able to thwart the distribution of the piece. As is the case with other change initiatives, the support of senior executives is critical to the success of motivational stories.

A story must be believable, realistic, and most importantly perceived as achievable. We are often asked if a story must be true. Before answering this very valid question, consider the following:

In 2006, Geena Davis won the Golden Globe Award for the Best Performance by an Actress in a Television Series—Drama. She won the award for her portrayal of the first woman to be president of the United States of America in the television show *Commander in Chief*. After being presented the award, she thanked the Hollywood Foreign Press and then stated, "As I was coming in, I felt a little tug on my skirt. I looked and there was a little girl, maybe 8 or ten, in her first party dress. She said, because of you, I want to be president some day." She paused while the audience, in unison, all said "awww" and then erupted into applause. The camera panned the audience, and many actors were teary-eyed with emotion over the story. She continued, "Well that didn't actually happen, but," she paused again. This time there was laughter and applause. She looked sheepish and then said, "Awww, but, it could have!" The audience laughed even harder, as she continued, "It very well could have, and if I was in the farmlands of Nebraska, or somewhere, there could have been a little girl, tugging at my dress. And were that to be the case, then all of this would be worth it."

Clearly, we do not suggest you make a habit of distorting the truth in your stories; however, as was the case with Geena Davis's acceptance speech, there are times when modest fabrications or white lies add incredible value, without creating harm. Much as Geena Davis did, we highly recommend that you remind your audience of your *stretching* of the truth once the point has been made. Returning to the original question, yes, stories should be true or based on the truth, at least in most cases. Of course, there will be times, especially in future-based stories where this is not always feasible or even desirable. For example, it is entirely acceptable to create future conditions to emphasize the point you are trying to make. We recommend that you follow the BRAT principle: Stories should be Believable, Realistic, Achievable, and based on the Truth. It is most important that you consider each of the elements.

Story Two—Guiding Faculty Into the Future

The second story was developed to excite change in an innovative Great Plains university (see Appendix 2). At the time, John was a new faculty member charged with the responsibility of integrating knowledge management into the core curriculum of the College of Business. This was no easy task, especially given the number of naysayers who were perfectly content with the status quo. One group believed knowledge management was just a passing fad and they had been involved with enough fads, thank you very much. A second group thought this *KM stuff* was a good idea, just as long as it did not affect them or their courses. The final group, which was the majority, had bought into the idea but did not really know what to do next.

The story was a mock interview with the dean 5 years hence. The story was *published* in a trade journal, titled *KM Today*, shortly after the College was the recipient of the Most Innovative Knowledge Educator (MIKE) award. In the interview, the dean described the implementation of the program and how it had improved the quality of education for the students. The final question asked by the interviewer was, "What would you do differently?" to which the dean replies, "I wish we would have started sooner." Grinning, he continued, "The success of the program makes me wish more folks could have benefited, had we started in 2003, we would have helped another cohort. That said I am absolutely delighted with our results."

Both the trade journal and the award in this story were fictitious, as were the other organizations mentioned in the accompanying stories. As a result, they resembled their real alter egos. For example, the genuine trade magazine is titled *KM World* (see http://www.kmworld.com), while the authentic award is the Most Admired Knowledge Enterprise (MAKE) (see http://www.knowledgebusiness.com). This allowed the story to be distributed as a *reprint* from the fictitious, though recognizable, trade journal.

Unlike the first story, this time the story focused on an individual, the dean, who was very well known in the organization. For this reason, the dean's real name was used, and with his permission his style was carefully modeled in the mock interview. This blending of the real and simulated worlds went some way in helping to convince the readers that the story was believable and achievable. Once again, a vital component of the story's success was executive support. The dean reviewed an early draft of the story, and he was delighted with the format and the message.

Story Three—Guiding Students Into the Future

Based on the success of the previous stories, John penned another future-based story (see Appendix 3). This time the target audience was a group of executive graduate students completing an accelerated Master of Science in Management program of which John was director. A key element to this program is a major research paper that must be completed before graduation. Historically, all students have completed the course work based on the published schedule; however, there tended to be a handful of students who procrastinated on the projects. This procrastination caught the attention of the university administrators who seemed worried that this tardiness may jeopardize the program. In the past, a variety of techniques were used to instill a sense of urgency in the students, but needless to say, the desired results were still not being achieved.

Once again, the use of narrative was selected as the way ahead. This time the story was set just months in the future, unlike the previous stories that were several years in the future. Specifically, the date of the story was the graduation date of the group with the following headline: "Class of 2005—The First Cohort to Graduate as a Group." The story was *published* in a newspaper with a striking resemblance to the university's student newspaper.

The target audience for this tale was a group of geographically separated students who needed a morale boost. The story was printed and mailed to the students' homes. At the end of the day, the story achieved its aim by helping focus the students on the few remaining months of the program. Several students commented that the story allowed them to see the light at the end of the tunnel. Ultimately, the class of 2005 was the first cohort to graduate as a group–we believe the story helped to achieve this milestone.

Moral of the Story

All good stories should end with a moral, and this story is no different. This saga began by reviewing the timeless story of a stonecutter and a cathedral builder. Given we believe that most executives would wish for an army of cathedral builders rather than stonecutters, we reviewed the literature to see what the gurus were suggesting. The literature is rich with examples of raconteurs guiding the way ahead with oral stories; however, the domain of written stories was far less mature.

After reviewing a trio of future-based written stories, we hope you agree the power of the pen may be as effective as a well-told oral story. In each case, the written word proved to be a powerful motivator by capturing the imagination and attention of the target audience. Perhaps these types of stories are not well suited to all audiences; however, for some groups the written word is more powerful than even the best oral story. To quote a faculty member who was initially against the change and now a supporter of the idea, "Now I get it." Just four words, but four words that mean one more team member is a supporter—those are four important words! The target audience seems to be a key to the success of these stories.

For some groups it is simply not possible to capture the attention of all group members with an oral rendition. This is certainly the case with the three groups described in this chapter. Two of the groups, the military and student groups, were separated geographically and it would have been extremely difficult to have them meet to hear the story. The majority of the third group, the faculty, were geographically collocated but as a group were not very receptive to a gathering to discuss the subject. Anecdotal evidence seems to support the premise that the target audiences for these stories prefer the written word to the spoken word.

The moral of this story is that both written and oral stories are effective tools in sharing organizational knowledge, sparking change, and guiding people into the future. The wise executive should consider both forms of stories to help guide their organizations.

Remember the Cathedral Builder

The classic *Cathedral Builder* story is an example of how a well-told story can motivate men and women to make great sacrifices if they believe their work is important. One can imagine that most leaders would wish to have a team of cathedral builders rather than stonecutters. Will such stories resonate in your organization?

Now You Know . . .

- Stories are a primary mode of human communication and thinking.
- There are seven types of stories used by leaders, including sparking action, communicating who you are, transmitting values, fostering collaboration, taming the grapevine, sharing knowledge, and leading people into the future (Denning, 2004).
- A crucial component of future-based stories' success is executive support.
- People do judge the book by the cover—make sure your future-based story is aesthetically pleasing.
- Stories should follow the BART principle—they should be Believable, Realistic, Achievable, and based on the Truth.
- A blending of the real and simulated worlds may help to convince the readers that the story was believable and achievable.

CHAPTER 8

The Future Is
Just a Day Away

The best thing about the future is that it comes only one day at a time.

—Abraham Lincoln

For the past two decades, public and private sector executives and managers have struggled to develop effective ways of sharing what their organizations know. Driven by concerns such as downsizing, the impending retirement of baby boomers, terrorism, the troubling economy, and a host of other organizational challenges, many leaders have sought ways to share knowledge with both internal and external stakeholders. For the past decade, much of their work was built on the solid foundation provided by several seminal works including *Working Knowledge* (Davenport & Prusak, 1998), *If Only We Knew What We Know* (O'Dell & Grayson, 1998), and *The Knowledge Creating Company* (Nonaka & Konno, 1998).

Despite the best efforts of many innovative leaders, few organizations have achieved the desired level of knowledge sharing. This is certainly not due to a lack of energy, enthusiasm, or excitement on the part of executives, but rather the result of technology-focused, complicated, and expensive tools, techniques, and technologies. Equally, a culture based on a *need-to-know* rather than one based on a *need-to-share basis* prevented the transparency necessary to achieve organizational knowledge goals.

Our review suggests that many first-generation knowledge management projects were based on collecting and classifying information. The belief seemed to be that if we developed huge, centralized, IT-based repositories of artifacts, then stakeholders would serve themselves. Unfortunately, this approach never delivered the promised user-friendly access but rather resulted in many very expensive partial databases of little value.

Second-generation knowledge management projects shifted the focus to codifying tacit knowledge and combining explicit knowledge to create new knowledge. This approach seemed plausible in theory; however, quickly it became apparent that codifying tacit knowledge was difficult and very expensive, both in terms of time and money. Further exacerbating the challenge was the issue of information overload that resulted from the combination efforts.

Today we are seeing some very promising results from third-generation knowledge projects, which focus on connecting people and facilitating collaboration. Some organizations are now reaping the benefits of using social media tools such as wikis for collaboration and knowledge-sharing and commercial social networking tools, such as Facebook, LinkedIn, Socialcast, or Twitter for connecting people. These emerging tools and techniques provide flexible, agile, and intuitive solutions for connecting people with people and facilitating coordination, communication, and collaboration.

A word of warning is necessary, as most of the tools, tactics, and techniques that we will discuss in this chapter are relatively immature. Indeed, this is a domain in which practitioners are leading and academics are lagging. As a result, there is little empirical research to support many of the claims articulated by the proponents. Unlike the ideas we covered in previous chapters, the ideas presented here are likely more suited to early adopters. We believe that each of the emerging concepts are worthy of consideration; however, caveat emptor—let the buyer (or user) beware!

Sagology

The more we analyze the first and second-generation knowledge management projects, the more we believe that we got exactly what we asked. In other words, it seems likely that collectively we were confused about what we really wanted. Let us use the concept of Expertise Location Systems (ELS) as an example. There are many great examples of ELS in action; however, there are few examples of ELS being institutionalize in large organizations. Most examples of successful ELS implementations are relatively small scale—small islands of knowledge management in a larger sea of chaos.

We believe that many projects relied too much on process rather than the enablers of technology, leadership, and culture. Returning to ELS, what we find is that the process works fine in theory. Simply develop a process where we can record everyone's expertise and then knowledge seekers will be able to, magically, connect with these knowledge providers. Unfortunately, this approach viewed knowledge *production* as a very mechanical process. In practice, many of the knowledge providers were too busy to bother with the system or were guilty of knowledge hoarding. In other words, we ignored the cultural component of knowledge management. Clearly, in the future we must consider the enablers, especially as they apply to our organization.

We also believe that sometimes leaders may have missed the point of the whole exercise. Earlier in the book, we offered Davenport and Prusak's definition of knowledge:

> a fluid mix of framed experience, values, contextual information, expert insight that provides a framework for evaluating and incorporating new experiences and information. It originates and is applied in the minds of knowers. In organizations, it often becomes embedded not only in documents or repositories but also in organizational routines, processes, practices, and norms. (Davenport & Prusak, 1998, p. 5)

The elevator version of this definition might be "concepts, experience, and insight that provide a framework for creating, evaluating and using information" (Laudon & Laudon, 2005, p. 373). We like this concise definition as it supports the concept of the cognitive hierarchy by suggesting that knowledge is about evaluating and using information. Despite the pleasing nature of this definition, we sometimes wonder if evaluating and using information is really the desired end state. Is that all executives need, evaluating and using information?

The same authors who eloquently penned our elevator definition of knowledge are proponents of the notion that the cognitive hierarchy extends beyond knowledge. In *Essentials of Management Information Systems: Managing the Digital Firm,* the authors, Kenneth and Jane Laudon, provided a clear, concise, and accurate definition for the apex of the knowledge pyramid. They define *wisdom* as "the collective and individual experiences of applying knowledge to the solution of problems" (Laudon & Laudon, 2005, p. 373). We like this definition because it brings two important ideas to the table. First is the notion that wisdom is derived from both individual and collective experiences, which reminds us that this is probably a team sport and not an individual effort. Equally important is the phase "applying knowledge to the solution of the problem." This concept is paramount as it reinforces our belief that many leaders will only embark on this knowledge journey to solve organizational challenges, present or future.

We often refer to this expanded hierarchy as the *Knowledge Edge*, which is the domain of senior leaders (see Figure 10). Compare this element to *Knowledge Creation*, which is often the area of expertise for middle managers or executive staff. Remember earlier that we described the methods for creating knowledge. We suggested there are five major ways to transform data into information. First, one may put the data into *context* by communicating the reason for gathering the data. Second, one may *categorize* the data by describing the breakdown or the essential components of the data. Third, one may mathematically or statistically *calculate* the data. Fourth, one may *correct* errors in previously reported data. Finally, one may *condense* the data by providing a summary instead of the entire collection of data. Equally, we argued there are four activities that transform information into the knowledge. First, one may *compare* information with previous information, primarily to determine what has changed in a particular situation. Second, one may determine the *consequences* or repercussions of this information on decisions. Third, one may consider how this information *connects* or correlates to other information. Finally, through *conversation* one may conclude what people think about the information (Davenport & Prusak, 1998).

Without wishing to dwell on definitions, we think it is important to realize that there is much more to knowledge management than the rather mechanical production of knowledge. Knowledge management, which many agree is a rather unfortunate term, is much more; it really is about senior leaders combining their organizational knowledge with experience to solve challenges. To emphasize the difference, we have adopted a different term for this essential executive function. We use the term *sagology*

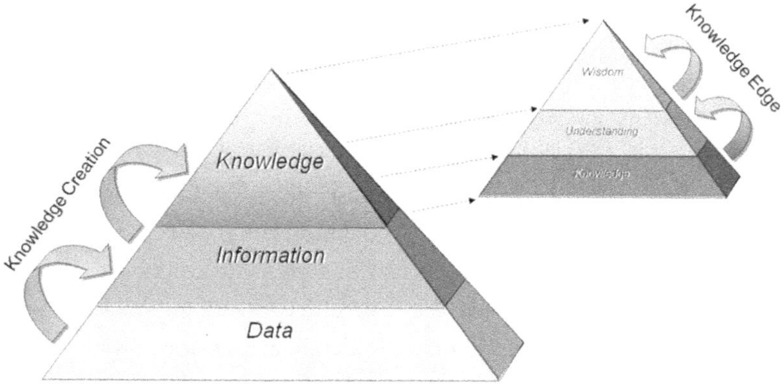

Figure 10. The Knowledge Edge

to describe our work, which we define as the study of organizational wisdom in all its forms, especially with reference to technology, leadership, culture, process, and measurement. The remainder of this chapter focuses on sagology and how leaders may apply the idea to their future needs.

The Power of the People

By far the most watched phenomenon of the 21st century surrounds the power of everyday people. Executives across the board seem surprised by the sudden, and sometimes unwanted, knowledge and resultant power of the people. In their book *Groundswell: Winning in a World Transformed by Social Technologies,* Forrester analysts Charlene Li and Josh Bernoff describe part of this phenomenon as a groundswell, which they define as "a social trend in which people use technologies to get the things they need from each other, rather than from traditional institutions like corporations" (Li & Bernoff, 2008, p. 9).

In a 2006 *Wired* magazine article, Jeff Howe coined the term crowd-sourcing to describe "everyday people using their spare cycles to create content, solve problems, even do corporate R & D" (Howe, 2006). In his book, *Crowdsourcing: Why the Power of the Crowd Is Driving the Future of Business,* Howe defined crowdsourcing as "the act of taking a job traditionally performed by a designated agent (usually an employee) and outsourcing it to an undefined, generally large group of people in the form of an open call" (Howe, 2008). Howe wrote, "The amount of knowledge and talent dispersed among the human race has always outstripped our capacity to harness it. Crowdsourcing corrects that—but in doing so, it also unleashes the forces of creative destruction" (Howe, 2008).

Both terms, groundswell and crowdsourcing, are neologisms and as a result many academics may dismiss them as hype designed to sell books. However, we would caution against a hasty dismissal. Of course, time will be the real test of their relevance. In the meantime, we suggest that leaders should learn about the opportunities and threats of the social revolution. We are most concerned about these ideas from a knowledge point of view and therefore we will not consider, in any great detail, the related marketing, public relations, or economic issues.

Digging Out of a Crisis

Both books we mentioned above, *Groundswell* and *Crowdsourcing*, include a story about a Web site called Digg.com—our version follows. The site was cofounded by an innovative young entrepreneur named Kevin Rose. In August 2006, Rose was featured on the cover of *Business Week* magazine with the caption, "How This Kid Made $60 Million in 18 Months" (Lacy & Hempel, 2006). Rose was one of the real pioneers of the social revolution; he was one of the first to capitalize on the power of people by allowing people to have a vote. Digg.com allows users from around the world to nominate their favorite stories on the Web. Once a *digger* nominates a story, its ranking on the site is determined by its popularity among diggers (the collective term for people who contribute to Digg .com)—the most popular story, which is based on Digg's proprietary ranking algorithm, will be at the top of the list.

On May Day 2007, a shot was fired that was heard around the virtual world; the shot caught the tech world's attention. Just one day before, the number one digg was a story that included a code to crack HD-DVDs. Given that such knowledge likely infringed copyright laws, the movie industry wanted the code removed and reluctantly the Digg team decided to remove the listing. Digg CEO Jay Adelson posted the following to the Digg Blog.

Digg Blog—May 1 2007, 1 PM (Adelson, 2007)

Hey all,

I just wanted to explain what some of you have been noticing around some stories that have been submitted to Digg on the HD DVD encryption key being cracked.

This has all come up in the past 24 hours, mostly connected to the HD-DVD hack that has been circulating online, having been posted to Digg as well as numerous other popular news and information Web sites. We've been notified by the owners of this intellectual property that they believe the posting of the encryption key infringes their intellectual property rights. In order to respect these rights and to comply with the law, we have removed postings of the key that have been brought to our attention.

Whether you agree or disagree with the policies of the intellectual property holders and consortiums, in order for Digg to survive, it must abide by the law. Digg's Terms of Use, and the terms of use of most popular sites, are required by law to include policies against the infringement of intellectual property. This helps protect Digg from claims of infringement and being shut down due to the posting of infringing material by others.

Our goal is always to maintain a purely democratic system for the submission and sharing of information—and we want Digg to continue to be a great resource for finding the best content. However, in order for that to happen, we all need to work together to protect Digg from exposure to lawsuits that could very quickly shut us down.

Thanks for your understanding,
Jay

Figure 11. Blog Entry by Digg CEO Jay Adelson

What happened next surprised almost everyone. Diggers from around the world re-dugg the story to ensure that it was number one. As quick as the story was removed, it was re-dugg to the top once again. This continued until the Digg.com site was taken off-line. Eight hours after Jay Adelson's post, Kevin Rose posted the following to the Digg Blog.

Digg Blog—May 1, 2007, 9 PM (Rose, 2007)

Today was an insane day. And as the founder of Digg, I just wanted to post my thoughts . . .

In building and shaping the site I've always tried to stay as hands on as possible. We've always given site moderation (digging/burying) power to the community. Occasionally we step in to remove stories that violate our terms of use (e.g., linking to pornography, illegal downloads, racial hate sites, etc.). So today was a difficult day for us. We had to decide whether to remove stories containing a single code based on a cease and desist declaration. We had to make a call, and in our desire to avoid a scenario where Digg would be interrupted or shut down, we decided to comply and remove the stories with the code.

But now, after seeing hundreds of stories and reading thousands of comments, you've made it clear. You'd rather see Digg go down fighting than bow down to a bigger company. We hear you, and effective immediately we won't delete stories or comments containing the code and will deal with whatever the consequences might be.

If we lose, then what the hell, at least we died trying.

Digg on,
Kevin

Figure 12. Blog Entry by Digg Cofounder Kevin Rose

The moral of this story became very clear, very quickly. Gone are the days when corporate leaders may control what knowledge is distributed, especially through the Internet. The power of the people, especially the network army of Web contributors, represents a force heretofore unknown. Finally, the cofounders of Digg.com learned a lesson that is changing the business world—the future is just a day away. Digg.com's leaders reacted quickly and decisively to the crisis, had they followed conventional thinking and timelines, Digg might not exist today. Organizational leaders must be aware of what is being said about their organizations on the Web, they must know the good, the bad, and the ugly—they must also be able to react quickly to the community's wants and needs.

The Social Revolution

The Digg crisis is a good example of changing knowledge environment and illustrates the power of the community. But what has changed to empower these communities with such power? Surely, groups of passionate people have long yearned for the opportunity to influence or perhaps even hijack issues. Of course, there have been many times in history when large groups congregated to spark change. However, the logistics with massing large groups can be very cumbersome, expensive, and difficult to communicate.

Enter Web 2.0—a World Wide Web based on collaboration rather than content—and suddenly all of these obstacles evaporate, at least for virtual groups. In their book Wikinomics: *How Mass Collaboration Changes Everything,* authors Dan Tapscott and Anthony Williams describe how a low-cost collaborative infrastructure is empowering the many—they term these "the weapons of mass collaboration" (Tapscott & Williams, 2006, p. 11). Tapscott and Williams warn these *weapons* support a new level of collaboration that will turn the economy upside down and may well facilitate the destruction of organizations who fail to adjust.

To understand the power of these new collaborative tools, consider the transformation of the travel industry. For many years, JoAnn worked in the travel business. JoAnn's business was all about knowledge and access to information, much of which she paid to access. Over time, she developed a clientele who knew JoAnn and trusted her judgment. They knew that she had incredible knowledge of many destinations and she had access to information, like wholesale prices, that was only available to the industry insiders. Today that has changed as most mere mortals now have more access to higher fidelity information, usually at no cost, than the professionals of just a couple of years ago. Through sites such as Tripadvisor.com, SeatGuru.com, Wikitravel.com, and Orbitz.com, to name just a few, we are now able to gain the valuable knowledge we need to make travel decisions.

Consider the following example from our recent trip to speak at an International Knowledge Management conference in Cape Town, South Africa. Whenever we travel to a new destination for business, we try to build in a little time to learn about the host country. We decided to arrive in Cape Town a few days early to tour the city and surrounding area. Our first real question was where to stay. A quick search on Tripadvisor.com revealed one particular guesthouse, *An African Villa*, received rave reviews from many people. In fact, virtually everyone who had stayed there rated the hotel as five stars, resulting in *An African Villa* being rated as the best hotel in Cape Town. In addition to the high quantitative scores the qualitative comments were glowing—most reviewers took the time to describe in detail just how happy they were with the property and the staff. Finally, we reviewed the photos provided by the many happy visitors. We thought this would be a great place to stay and decided to book. We made this decision because we trusted the 100 or so people who had provided feedback to Tripadvisor.com.

Our next challenge was to decide what to do before the conference. We only had a couple of days to see the sights so we decided it would be best to hire a guide for our visit. We searched several travel sites but did not find any guides that seemed to meet our needs. We decided to contact An African Villa and ask their advice. Suddenly we were treating An African Villa as a trusted authority as we assumed that they would not recommend anyone who might negatively influence our experience and ultimately our rating of the hotel. Within a day, we had an e-mail recommending a couple who were certified guides. One more e-mail and we were set. As it turns out, we could not have been happier with either the property or our guide. This is an example of the power of collaboration and knowledge sharing. Through the collective knowledge of many Tripadvisor.com contributors, none of whom is paid for their services, we gained invaluable insight to make our decision. Frankly, it would be virtually impossible for a professional travel consultant in our home city to be able to provide this service.

Social Media Knowledge-Sharing Tools

There are many examples of how organizations are using the collaborative forces of the Internet to create and exchange knowledge. The question is, What are you doing in your organization to exploit the weapons of mass collaboration? Virtually every day, new Web tools are being developed offering new ways to foster collaboration and knowledge sharing. Our aim is not to endorse particular tools, but rather to encourage leaders to think about how these tools will help them achieve a competitive advantage. Below is a brief summary of three tools worthy of notice—please remember this list was current as of early 2009, and almost certainly there will be new entrants very soon. We encourage you to learn about social media and decide what tools are best suited to your needs.

Crowdsourcing

Earlier we provided Howe's definition of crowdsourcing: "the act of taking a job traditionally performed by a designated agent (usually an employee) and outsourcing it to an undefined, generally large group of people in the form of an open call" (Howe, 2008). One great example of this idea in practice is the InnoCenter (see http://www.innocenter.com), which aims to connect "companies, academic institutions, public sector and non-profit organizations, all hungry for breakthrough innovation, with a global network of more than 160,000 of the world's brightest mind"

("InnoCenter About Us," 2009). By connecting knowledge seekers with knowledge solvers, crowdsourcing may be a way for organizations to gain knowledge from outside sources that would be very expensive to develop in-house. Could this help you solve organizational challenges?

Social Networking

The single largest cultural-technological innovation of the 21st century is the social networking Web site. These sites help people connect with other people to collaborate in an online environment. Some are designed for connecting friends and family (e.g., Facebook or MySpace), while others facilitate professional connection (e.g., LinkedIn). Here we are, just a few years into the new millennium, and it is hard to remember what the world was like before Facebook (founded 2004), MySpace (founded 2003), or LinkedIn (founded 2003).

 According to Alexa.com, a Web traffic–ranking site, Facebook was the fifth most popular site on the planet with a daily reach of nearly 15% of global Web users (based on January 13, 2009 data). How can you use social networking?

Wikis

Wikis are the epitome of what many people think of Web 2.0—a collaborative Web page that is quick and easy to edit. In fact, the name "Wiki" is a Hawaiian word meaning *fast*. By far the best known example of a wiki is the infamous Wikipedia, the self-proclaimed free encyclopedia. During a recent fund-raising campaign, Wikipedia founder Jimmy Wales wrote,

> Wikipedia is driven by a global community of more than 150,000 volunteers—all dedicated to sharing knowledge freely. Over almost eight years, these volunteers have contributed more than 11 million articles in 265 languages. More than 275 million people come to our website every month to access information, free of charge and free of advertising. But Wikipedia is more than a website. We share a common cause: *Imagine a world in which every single person on the planet is given free access to the sum of all human knowledge. That's our commitment.* (Wales, 2008, p. 1)

Consider the impact of Wales's second to last sentence at the micro level; imagine how this might work in your organization. Perhaps your vision might be *Imagine an organization in which every single person on the team is given free access to the sum of all organizational knowledge.* A wiki might be a very low-cost, high-return tool for collaboration and knowledge sharing in your organization.

Remember Kevin Rose

Kevin Rose, cofounder of Digg.com, is one of the real pioneers of the social revolution; he was one of the first to capitalize on the power of people by allowing people to have a vote. Equally important, he reacted quickly and decisively to the Digg crisis of 2007; had Kevin Rose followed conventional thinking and timelines, Digg might not exist today. Organizational leaders must be aware of what is being said about their organizations on the Web; they must know the good, the bad, and the ugly. They must also be able to react quickly to the community's wants and needs.

Now You Know . . .

- **Crowdsourcing** is the act of taking a job traditionally performed by a designated agent (usually an employee) and outsourcing it to an undefined, generally large group of people in the form of an open call (Howe, 2008).
- **Groundswell** is a social trend in which people use technologies to get the things they need from each other, rather than from traditional institutions like corporations (Li & Bernoff, 2008, p. 12).
- **Knowledge** (the elevator version) is the concepts, experience, and insight that provide a framework for creating, evaluating, and using information (Laudon & Laudon, 2005, p. 373).
- **Sagology** is the study of organizational wisdom in all its forms, especially with reference to technology, leadership, culture, process, and measurement.
- **Wisdom** is the collective and individual experiences of applying knowledge to the solution of problems (Laudon & Laudon, 2005, p. 373).
- The future starts now.

Key Terms

After Action Review, or AAR, is a post-event knowledge collection process, which considers four questions:

1. What was supposed to happen?
2. What happened?
3. What is the difference?
4. What should we do to improve?

Ba can be thought of as a shared space for emerging relationships. This space can be physical (e.g., office, dispersed business space), virtual (e.g., e-mail, teleconference), mental (e.g., shared experiences, ideas, ideals), or any combination of them. What differentiates *ba* from ordinary human interaction is the concept of knowledge creation. *Ba* provides a platform for advancing individual and/or collective knowledge. It is from such a platform that a transcendental perspective integrates all information needed (Nonaka & Konno, 1998).

BRAT is a story writing principle that suggests stories should be Believable, Realistic, Achievable, and based on the Truth.

Cartographic School is a component of Michael Earl's knowledge management taxonomy. The purpose of this school is to make sure knowledgeable people in the organization are accessible to others for advice, consultation, or knowledge exchange (Earl, 2001).

Combination is the transfer of explicit knowledge to explicit knowledge. Through the process of codification, one person may document specific knowledge into some form of repository so that many others may access knowledge. An organization developing and formalizing best practices is a classic example of transferring explicit knowledge. Equally common is the creation of new knowledge by combining previously documented explicit knowledge (Nonaka & Takeuchi, 1995).

Commercial School is a component of Michael Earl's knowledge management taxonomy. It is overtly and explicitly concerned with both protecting and exploiting a firm's knowledge or intellectual assets to produce revenue streams (Earl, 2001).

Community of Practice is a place where people generate new knowledge that increases stocks and facilitates the flow of knowledge capital in an organization (Saint-Onge & Wallace, 2003).

Crowdsourcing is a neologism describing everyday people using their spare cycles to create content, solve problems, and even do corporate R & D (Howe, 2006).

Data is a set of discrete, objective facts about events; in an organizational context, data is most usefully described as structured records of transactions (Davenport & Prusak, 1998).

Engineering School is a component of Michael Earl's knowledge management taxonomy that focuses on two related concepts. The first is that performance of business processes can be enhanced by providing operating personnel with knowledge relevant to their task and second that management processes are inherently more knowledge-intensive than business processes (Earl, 2001).

Enterprise Dementia is a debilitating organizational ailment that comprises two closely related components: information anxiety and organizational memory loss (Girard, 2005c).

Explicit Knowledge is "formal and specific . . . [and] can be easily communicated and shared" (Nonaka, 1991).

Externalization is the transfer of tacit knowledge to the explicit form. For example, one may wish to articulate or externalize the highly personal knowledge of a master artisan into an explicit form that is easier to formalize or document (Nonaka & Takeuchi, 1995).

Failure to Capture is failing to incorporate new knowledge into the broader organizational memory (de Holan et al., 2004).

Groundswell is a neologism describing a social trend in which people use technologies to get the things they need from each other rather than from traditional institutions like corporations (Li & Bernoff, 2008).

Information is a message, usually in the form of a document or an audible or visible communication. Fundamental to this definition is the underlying assumption that a message must have a sender and a receiver. Information is meant to change the way the receiver perceives something, to have an impact on his judgment and behavior (Davenport & Prusak, 1998).

Information Anxiety is the black hole between data and knowledge. It happens when information doesn't tell us what we want or need to know. The five components of information anxiety are

1. not understanding information;
2. feeling overwhelmed by the amount of information to be understood;
3. not knowing if certain information exists;
4. not knowing where to find information; and
5. knowing exactly where to find the information, but not having the key to access it (Wurman, 1989).

Information Overload occurs when the amount of input to a system exceeds its processing capacity (Speier et al., 1999). Alternatively, information overload is described as that state in which available, and potentially useful, information is a hindrance rather than a help (Bawden, 2001).

Internalization is the transfer of explicit knowledge to the tacit form. The premise is knowledge creation through an amalgamation of codified explicit knowledge and fuzzy tacit knowledge. Consider the master artisan who educates himself in the sciences and through this education and his intuition is able to develop a better way to produce his craft (Nonaka & Takeuchi, 1995).

Knowledge is a fluid mix of framed experience, values, contextual information, and expert insight that provides a framework for evaluating and incorporating new experiences and information. It originates and is applied in the minds of knowers. In organizations, it often becomes embedded not only in documents or repositories but also in organizational routines, processes, practices, and norms (Davenport & Prusak, 1998).

Knowledge Workers have high degrees of expertise, education, or experience, and the primary purpose of their jobs involves the creation, distribution, or application of knowledge (Davenport, 2005).

Memory Decay is the accidental loss of existing organizational knowledge (de Holan et al., 2004).

Organizational Alzheimer's is memory loss that occurs when key employees leave an organization, taking their (tacit) knowledge with them (Galt, 2002).

Organizational Information Overload is a situation in which the extent of perceived information overload is sufficiently widespread within an organization as to reduce the overall effectiveness of management operations (Wilson, 2001).

Organizational School is a component of Michael Earl's knowledge management taxonomy that focuses on the use of organizational structures or networks to share or pool knowledge (Earl, 2001).

Personal Information Overload as a perception on the part of the individual (or observers of that person) that the flow of information associated with work tasks is greater than can be managed effectively (Wilson, 2001).

Sagology is the study of organizational wisdom in all its forms, especially with reference to technology, leadership, culture, process, and measurement.

SALT is an acronym for Same As Last Time.

Socialization is the transfer of tacit to tacit knowledge. Through social interaction, people may gain highly personal and difficult-to-formalize knowledge. One of the best examples is the apprentice shadowing the master artisan. Almost through osmosis, the young journeyperson learns the craft of the master. He or she will probably not understand the scientific principles underlying the master's skill, but through socialization, the student slowly gains the knowledge required to replicate the teacher (Nonaka & Takeuchi, 1995).

Spatial School is a component of Michael Earl's knowledge management taxonomy that provides a design for emergence philosophy of knowledge management. It centers on the use of space or spatial designs to facilitate knowledge exchange (Earl, 2001).

Strategic School is a component of Michael Earl's knowledge management taxonomy that sees knowledge management as a dimension of competitive strategy (Earl, 2001).

System School is a component of Michael Earl's knowledge management taxonomy designed to capture specialist knowledge in knowledge bases that other specialist or qualified people can access (Earl, 2001).

Tacit Knowledge is highly personal and hard to formalize, making it difficult to communicate and to share with others. Subjective insights, intuitions, and hunches all fall into this category of knowledge. Furthermore, tacit knowledge is deeply rooted in an individual's action and experience, as well as in the ideals, values, or emotions he or she embraces (Nonaka & Takeuchi, 1995).

Unlearning is when a company intentionally removes something that is well established in the organization's memory (de Holan et al., 2004).

Wisdom is the collective and individual experiences of applying knowledge to the solution of problems (Laudon & Laudon, 2005, p. 373).

Appendix A

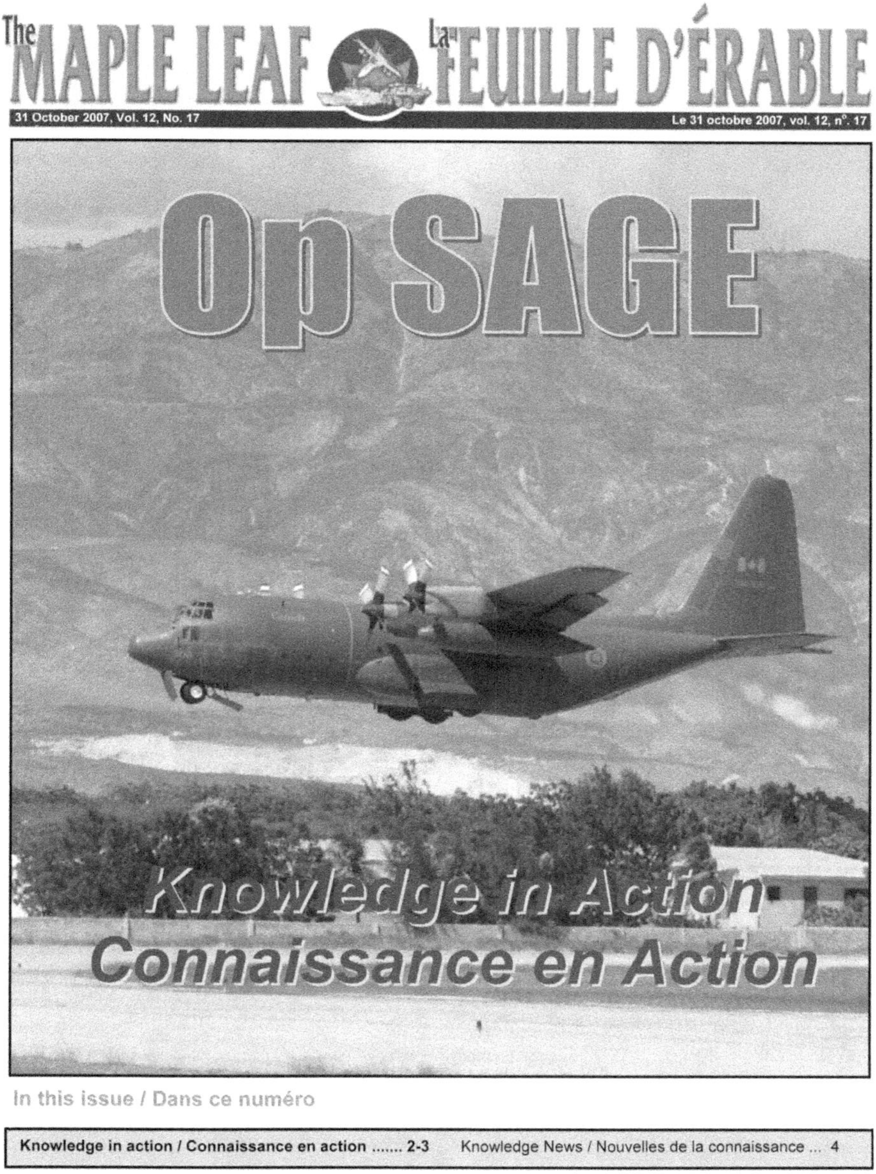

The MAPLE LEAF La FEUILLE D'ÉRABLE

31 October 2007, Vol. 12, No. 17 Le 31 octobre 2007, vol. 12, n°. 17

Op SAGE

Knowledge in Action

Connaissance en Action

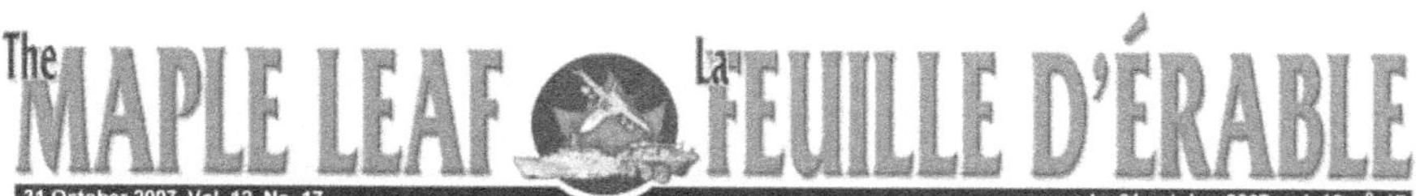

In this issue / Dans ce numéro

Knowledge in action / Connaissance en action .... 2-3 Knowledge News / Nouvelles de la connaissance ... 4

*This **fictitious** story describes the power of knowledge management in action.*
*It was created with the kind permission of the **Maple Leaf**.*

Twelve hours of Knowledge:
How knowledge sharing helped Op SAGE

(Ottawa) On Monday 29 October 2007, the Canadian Forces' Humanitarian Emergency Relief Team (HERT) arrived in Haiti to help the island nation deal with the aftermath of a natural disaster. HERT was the first international force to answer Haiti's call for assistance. This speedy response, called Operation SAGE, was made possible by connecting people with people to share knowledge. Their story is below.

On Sunday, the Commanding Officer (CO) HERT awoke to the ringing of his personal data assistant. It was 0615 and his Operations Officer had just sent him a priority email. The note contained a news feed describing a hurricane, which suddenly changed course and was heading toward the small Caribbean island nation of Haiti. The CO was surprised by the news as he and his team had been watching the storm for a number of days and most experts believed the storm would not reach land.

After reading the note, CO HERT opened his tablet PC, inserted his Public Key Infrastructure (PKI) card and turned on his computer. Within minutes, through a wireless connection, the CO's personal knowledgespace appeared, which included a dashboard showing the status of his unit. The dashboard was a collection of critical data and information maintained by his staff. The presentation of knowledge in an intuitive manner allowed the CO to quickly decide if he needed to take action or make any decisions. He was delighted to determine that his command group was available, less one officer who was leading a reconnaissance team on another Caribbean island.

Next, he read news from several sites reporting on the conditions in Haiti and the weather forecast for the next 72 hours. Sensing that this may be a mission for the HERT, he created a collaborative workspace for the contingency operation. The content of the workspace was based on the lessons learned from previous missions. After each mission, an After-action Review (AAR) identified the deficiencies and helped redefine the requirements of the workspace.

Returning to his knowledgespace, the CO typed the words *CF operations Haiti* and quickly rediscovered that the CF deployed to Haiti in 1997 and 2004. A synopsis of each operation was available as well as a series of links. To ensure this information was readily available to the other members of his team, he dragged the links into the contingency collaborative workspace. He also saw a list of *experts* on Haiti, including a policy officer from Western Hemisphere Policy, a member of the intelligence staff, a lawyer from Director of International Law and others. He added the list of names to the collaborative workspace.

Eye of the hurricane over Haiti

Next, he opened the staff list for the 1997 operation, but he did not recognize any of the names; in any case, he dragged the link to the staff list into the collaborative workspace. He decided to connect to the CF People Finder application to see where the 1997 battlegroup commander was now. Before being given access to the application, his profile was reviewed to see if he should be given access to the sensitive data. This is a relatively new improvement to the People Finder. In the past he would have had to contact ADM(HR-Mil) to gain access to the information. However, in 2005 decided that a more trusted environment was necessary to support operations. To guard against potential abuses, a sophisticated algorithm monitors all accesses to the People Finder and will lock out and report abusers.

The CO determined that the battlegroup commander retired in 2006 as brigadier-general; however, he remained a member of the Supplementary Reserve and had agreed to be contacted for operational reasons. CO HERT added these details to the collaborative workspace. When he clicked on the 2004 staff list, he was surprised to find that a Staff College friend of his was the deputy commanding officer of the operation. Using People Finder, he determined that his friend is in Ottawa – this fact was added to the workspace.

The CO saw a small flashing icon beside his friend's name, indicating that he was online. Clicking on this icon an Instant Messaging (IM) box appeared and he typed a quick note to his friend. He asked if his friend had heard about the storm and received a quick response saying "AFK – WIMU 10" – which of course is shorthand for "I am away from my keyboard, I will instant message you in 10 minutes" – such shorthand is used when one is using a cellular telephone or other handheld device.

While waiting for his friend to return the IM, he clicked on a link to the lessons learned library. The genesis of the library was an idea from a Community of Practice in 2005. With members from a variety of organizations that collect and analyse lessons, for example the Army Lesson Learned Centre, Director General Safety, Flight Safety, the community thought it would be a great idea to share information amongst each other. The

Director Knowledge Management built on this great idea by sponsoring a project to consolidate the various sources. Today with a click of a button, the CO is able to search a variety of knowledge stores.

The lessons learned library produced some very important lessons. First, he noted that during the 2004 operation, the battlegroup had problems using floppy disks to store data. It turns out that the sand from the island was corrupting the magnetic medium. Their solution was to use Universal Serial Bus (USB) thumb drives in lieu of floppy disks. Next, he discovered that in 1997 there had been a problem with the Status of Forces Agreement (SOFA) for the neighbouring country of Cuba. Other issues were also highlighted, all of which were moved to the collaborative workspace and flagged for the Operations Officer's attention. The SOFA issue was a priority so it triggered an automatic message to the Operations Officer, who reviewed the message and prepared a note to the lawyer identified by the CO as an authority in the area.

It was now 1000 and the CO's staff college friend sent him an IM. He asked his friend a number of questions about the previous operation. After a few minutes, the CO received an IM from the COS J3 in Ottawa suggesting a Warning Order was being developed and would likely be signed off before noon. The CO parted company with his friend and they agree that if anything else developed they would *talk* again.

The CO sent an IM inviting COS J3 into the collaborative workspace and he provided an overview of his morning. COS J3 remarked that *he did not know how they did it in the old days*. He suggested that the CO drive from Kingston to Ottawa for an afternoon classified briefing – they agreed to meet at 1600. The CO signed out of his knowledgespace to tend to some personal issues before departing for Ottawa.

At 1120, the CO received a priority message on his cellular phone. The message was from the collaborative workspace and it stated that COS J3 had just uploaded the warning order. The CO signed into his knowledgespace, received the order, added some additional information and forwarded a message to his operations officer who knew exactly what to do based on standing operating procedures.

HERT's base camp in Haiti

At 1200, he grabbed his tablet PC along with a few other necessities and commenced the drive to Ottawa. At 1315, he was hit head-on by another vehicle and died instantly. At 1400, the COS J3 was notified of the tragic accident. After ensuring that all necessary arrangements were in place to help the CO's family, the COS J3 returned his attention to the operational mission at hand. Clearly, a new CO had to be appointed as the Prime Minister had just announced that the CF would be despatching the HERT within 24 hours.

The selection of the new CO was simple. Since 2006, the CF policy had been that all command positions must have identified successors. The nominated successor is informed of their selection and therefore is able to mentally prepare for transition. In this case, the successor was aware of her assumption of command in ten months and she had begun preparing to be a CO. Knowing that she would be the next CO, she had been thinking about the storm and wondering if HERT would be involved. She had also been thinking what she would do if she were CO. She remembered visiting the HERT in Kingston and being briefed on contingency plans.

The new CO HERT was informed of her new position at 1500. As she lived in Ottawa, she was able to meet with the COS J3 later that day. In the meantime, she was given access to the collaboration space and was able to review her predecessor's work. She too, knew the battlegroup commander from 2004 and decided to make contact. The two agreed to discuss the impending mission. As soon as they met face-to-face, the CO realized that her friend was uncomfortable about something. Soon he began to describe the details of a tragic incident on the island. The sharing of this experience would turn out to be very important in the days ahead. In fact, the story was so powerful that the CO never forgot the words of wisdom from her friend. After the operation, during the after-action review, she noted that the *war story* had saved the lives of several soldiers – that is the power of sharing knowledge.

At 1815, CO HERT met with the COS J3, just 12 hours after her processor first heard about the disaster. She told COS J3 that she was up to speed and ready to go. HERT deployed the next morning.

The speed of response for Op SAGE was the result of the COs' ability to rapidly connect to the data, information and knowledge they needed to make decisions and take actions – this is the essence of knowledge management. This is a story of the synergy of technology, leadership and culture; this is a story of the power of sharing.

About this Story

This is a fictitious story that describes the power of knowledge management in action. It was created with the permission of the managing editor of the **Maple Leaf**.

For More Information

For more information about using stories to spark organizational change please contact
Dr. John Girard
(john@johngirard.net).
Please contact Dr. Girard if you wish to distribute this story.

Version Française

Il y a une version française de cette histoire, demandez au Dr. Girard
(john@johngirard.net)

Appendix B

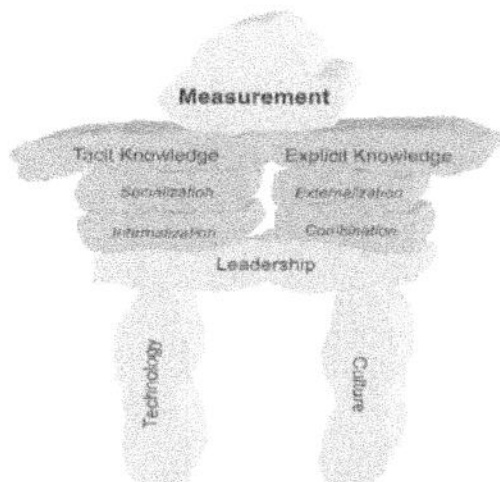

KM TODAY

KNOWLEDGE Management

SPECIAL EDITION: HIGHER EDUCATION

JULY / AUGUST 2008

The Inukshuk: A view from the North - page 12

Minot State University: Leader in *Applied* Knowledge Management

Dr. Roderic Hewlett, Dean of Minot State University's College of Business (www.minotstateu.edu), described "applied Knowledge Management as core *business* for faculty and students alike." Dean Hewlett recalled that "in the early days [2004] some people questioned the value of the program; however, four years later, virtually everyone is united in the view that the program has added incredible value."

Today, most students and faculty are members of at least one community of practice or interest, and students participate in after action reviews, collaborate virtually, and spark change through storytelling. According to Dean Hewlett "the applied aspect of the [KM] program is built on a solid academic foundation. Rather than simply exposing students to the theories of knowledge management, we create an environment in which we all may practice what we preach."

In addition to offering graduate and undergraduate knowledge management courses, Hewlett stated that "KM learner outcomes are integrated into many courses in the College." He proudly stated "that our combination of theory and practice provides a world class learning environment, one which is second to none." Dean Hewlett is confident that

MSU continues on page 2

RRU Renews Online KM MA

The Director of Knowledge Management programs at Royal Rivers University, Victoria, BC, has confirmed that RRU will continue its knowledge management (KM) Masters of Arts program. The revised online program will build on the highly acclaimed package offered by RRU for more than a decade. New to the program will be an emphasis on the post-Nokana period espoused by

RRU continues on page 7

Knowledge Management Modeling Research Continues at GWU

Great Western University's (GWU) Lead Professor for Knowledge Management (KM) announced that GWU will continue its ground breaking research in knowledge management. A team of researchers will investigate the relationships between leadership, organization, technology, and learning. Early results are expected in the summer or fall of 2009

GWU continues on page 3

#3459697/23 5682   *Postage paid in USA*

DR. JOHN GIRARD
MINOT STATE UNIVERSITY
500 UNIVERSITY AVE W
MINOT, ND 58703

In This Issue:

KM World
Supplement
Knowledge in Education

Industry watch 6
Corporate taxonomy 8
University review 14
Personal toolkit 26

MSU (continued from page 1)

students are benefitting from the College's profound commitment to knowledge management

". . . our combination of theory and practice provides a world class learning environment"

Minot State's journey toward a knowledge environment commenced in 2003 when Hewlett rallied the Faculty to endorse three themes for the College. Two of the themes were well known at MSU: International Business and Entrepreneurship - in each of these domains MSU was an acknowledged leader, much as is the case today. Hewlett recalls that "The third, knowledge management, was less well understood; nevertheless, the Faculty collectively agreed that the foundations of KM were sound and we agreed that KM should become a College theme."

Over the next year the College recruited a KM faculty member to take the lead in the development of the core KM program. One the first tasks was to ensure that the team understood the tenets of knowledge management. Hewlett recalled "KM was new to many Faculty. We decided to offer some awareness seminars - these turned out to be very successful and really helped our team understand why it was important to integrate knowledge management into the College's core curriculum."

During the awareness seminars the Minot State team agreed on a clear, concise definition for KM. Simply stated, they believe *KM is creating and sharing organizational knowledge.* Although more than fifty definitions could be found in the literature, the MSU team desired a simple definition to help guide the

development of their program.

Unlike many KM programs of the early 2000s, MSU decided not to design a bespoke KM degree, but rather, opted to incorporate the knowledge theories, tools and techniques into all College of Business programs. Although commonplace today, such a novel concept was unheard of only four years ago. MSU's pioneering efforts are likely the reason this best-practice has been successfully replicated across America.

Time has proven Hewlett correct, as an after-action-review, or AAR in the KM parlance, clearly demonstrated earlier this year. AARs are now routine events at MSU: instructors use the tool to validate learner outcomes, students are encouraged to participate in AARs to improve the quality of programs, and the administration use AARs to ensure programs are meeting the stated goals. For example, the AAR of the KM theme demonstrated conclusively that students, faculty, and the administration were benefitting from the creative project.

KM is creating and sharing organizational knowledge.

Hewlett uses Storytelling as an example of how the applied nature of KM has been incorporated. The College's core Business Communication Course includes a module on the theory of Storytelling, which is team-taught by two faculty members - one an expert in communications and the other in KM - together they provide a unique combination of experience. But it does not stop there, as students are expected to apply the concept of storytelling in Senior courses, such as the College's International Management course. Hewlett is convinced that "the blended teaching

approach combining the incremental application of tools and techniques is a recipe for success."

"KM learner outcomes are integrated into many courses in the College."

When asked what he would do differently, Hewlett paused reflectively, and then stated "I wish we would have started sooner." Grinning, he continued: "the success of the program makes me wish more folks could have benefitted, had we started in 2003, we would have helped another cohort. That said, I am absolutely delighted with our results."

The College of Business' innovative program earned MSU the distinction of being the 2008 MIKE (Most Innovative Knowledge Educator) Award recipient for their outstanding application of knowledge management in an educational environment. When accepting the award, Dean Hewlett offered to share the secrets of their success with others.

About this Story

This is a *fictitious* story that describes the power of knowledge management in action.

For More Information

For more information about storytelling to spark change in your organization, contact Dr. John Girard:

john@johngirard.net

Use of this Story

The author is a believer in sharing ideas; however, he would like to know who is using his stories. Please contact Dr. Girard if you wish to distribute this story.

Appendix C

SEEN & HEARD
MSU College of Business' Student Newspaper

CONGRATULATIONS JOB CORPS EXECUTIVE MANAGEMENT PROGRAM GRADUATES!

12 MAY 2006 — MINOT STATE UNIVERSITY — SPECIAL EDITION

Conference a Huge Success

"An overwhelming success" is how Dr. John Girard, the Director of Job Corps Executive Management Program (JCEMP), described the recent JCEMP research conference. "I am absolutely delighted with the quality of research completed by the JCEMP Fellows," stated Girard. Asked if he was surprised by the quality, Girard grinned and replied "Not at all - I would have been disappointed if the Fellows had not exceeded the standard normally expected of graduate students." He continued "this was a very motivated group; early in the year they decided to work as a team to ensure all Fellows completed high quality academic research projects."

Dr. Linda Cresap, Dean of the Graduate School, described the conference "as a huge success," and said "I hope this [conference] will become an annual event and perhaps even a model for other graduate programs."

In total twelve JCEMP Fellows presented the results of their research to a panel of College of Business faculty members and Minot business leaders. After each oral presentation the Fellows were subjected to a battery of questions by the panel.

Class of 2006 - The First JCEMP Cohort to Graduate as a Group

For the first time in the history of the Job Corps Executive Management Program (JCEMP) all Fellows graduated as a cohort. The twelve members of the Class of 2006 commenced their journey in June of last year by attending a five-week session here in Minot. All twelve returned to Minot this week for the today's Commencement ceremony, also a first for the program.

Dr. Gary Ross, Dean of the College of Business, described the milestone "as a tremendous achievement and a testament to the group's hard work, dedication and commitment." Ross described the Class as "an exceptional group of individuals that transformed into a high performance team."

After the Graduation ceremony the Program Director, Dr. John Girard, was seen *Job Corps hugging* each of the graduates, fulfilling a promise he made if the group graduated togther. He commented that "he was very proud of each and every graduate."

Speaking under the condition of anonymity, a group of graduates reported that the program was "easy peasy lemon squeezey" and that the "**praw**ject **prezen**tations were the best part of the course **eh!**" Dr. Girard suggested "they were speaking gibberish - obviously a result of stress."

References

Ackoff, R. L. (1994). *The democratic corporation: A radical prescription for recreating corporate America and rediscovering success.* New York: Oxford University Press.

Adelson, J. (2007). What's happening with HD-DVD stories? Retrieved January 8, 2009, from http://blog.digg.com/?p=73

Allee, V. (1997). *The knowledge evolution: Expanding organizational intelligence.* Boston: Butterworth-Heinemann.

Allee, V. (2003). *The future of knowledge: Increasing prosperity through value networks.* Amsterdam; Boston: Butterworth-Heinemann.

Allen, K. (2005). Organizational storytelling. *Franchising World, 37*(11), 63–64.

Baum, D. (2000). *Lightning in a bottle: Proven lessons for leading change.* Chicago: Dearborn.

Bawden, D. (2001). Information overload. *Library & Information Briefings, 92.*

Bell, S. (2004, April 2). Trust vital for e-commerce. *Computerworld (New Zealand).*

Bennet, A., & Bennet, D. (2004). *Organizational survival in the new world: The intelligent complex adaptive system.* Amsterdam; Boston: Butterworth-Heinemann.

Bontis, N. (2001). CKO wanted—evangelical skills necessary: A review of the Chief Knowledge Officer position. *Knowledge and Process Management, 8*(1), 29–38.

Boyett, J. H., & Boyett, J. T. (2001). *The guru guide to the knowledge economy: The best ideas for operating profitably in a hyper-competitive world.* New York: Wiley.

Buckman, R. H. (2004). *Building a knowledge-driven organization.* New York: McGraw-Hill.

Calabrese, F. A. (2000). *A suggested framework of key elements defining effective enterprise knowledge management programs.* Unpublished dissertation, George Washington University—District of Columbia.

Chartier, B., LaPointe, S., & Bonner, K. (2005). Get real—the art and power of storytelling in workplace communities. (Vol. 2006): Canada: Her Majesty the Queen in Right of Canada.

Chatzkel, J. (2002). Conversation with Alex Bennet, former deputy CIO for enterprise integration at the U.S. Department of Navy. *Journal of Knowledge Management, 6*(5), 434–444.

Complex. (2009). In Merriam-Webster online dictionary. Retrieved March 11, 2009, from http://www.merriam-webster.com/dictionary/complex

Crainer, S. (1997). *The ultimate book of business quotations.* Oxford: Capstone.

Davenport, T. H. (2005). *Thinking for a living: How to get better performance and results from knowledge workers.* Boston: Harvard Business School Press.

Davenport, T. H., & Prusak, L. (1998). *Working knowledge: How organizations manage what they know.* Boston: Harvard Business School Press.

de Holan, P. M., & Phillips, N. (2004). Remembrance of things past? The dynamics of organizational forgetting. *Management Science, 50*(11), 1603–1613.

de Holan, P. M., Phillips, N., & Lawrence, T. B. (2004). Managing organizational forgetting [Cover story]. *MIT Sloan Management Review, 45*(2), 45–51.

De Long, D. W. (2004). *Lost knowledge: Confronting the threat of an aging workforce.* Oxford; New York: Oxford University Press.

Denning, S. (2001). *The springboard: How storytelling ignites action in knowledge-era organizations.* Boston: Butterworth-Heinemann.

Denning, S. (2004). Telling tales. *Harvard Business Review, 82*(5), 122–129.

Denning, S. (2005, October). Mastering the discipline of business narrative. *Strategy & Leadership.*

DeTienne, K. B., & Jackson, L. A. (2001). Knowledge management: Understanding theory and developing strategy. *Competitiveness Review, 11*(1), 1–11.

DoD News Briefing—Secretary Rumsfeld and Gen. Myers. (2002, February 12). Retrieved July 6, 2006, from http://www.defenselink.mil/transcripts/2002/t02122002_t212sdv2.html

Drucker, P. F. (1988). The coming of the new organization. *Harvard Business Review, 66*(1), 45.

Earl, M. (2001). Knowledge management strategies: Toward a taxonomy. *Journal of Management Information Systems, 18*(1), 215–233.

Farrell, B. S. (2008). *The department of defense's civilian human capital strategic plan does not meet most statutory requirements.* Retrieved from http://www.gao.gov/new.items/d08439r.pdf

Feldman, S. (2004). The high cost of not finding information. *KM World, 13*(3), 8.

FM 100-6: Information operations. (1996). Washington, DC.

Forman, J. (1999). When stories create an organization's future. *Briefs* (15), 1–4.

Foster, L. G. (1983). The Johnson & Johnson credo and the Tylenol crisis. *New Jersey Bell Journal, 6*(1), 6.

Fulmer, W. E. (1999). Buckman laboratories (a). *Harvard Business School Cases,* 1–16.

Galt, V. (2002, February 22). Firms capture staff knowledge. *The Globe and Mail.*

Girard, J. P. (2004a). Defence knowledge management: Just a passing fad? *Canadian Military Journal, 5*(2), 17–27.

Girard, J. P. (2004b). *Toward an understanding of enterprise dementia: An empirical examination of information anxiety amongst public service middle managers.* Unpublished dissertation, Touro University International.

Girard, J. P. (2005a). Combating information anxiety: A management responsibility. *Organizaciju Vadyba: Sisteminiai Tyrimai, 35*(1), 65–79.

Girard, J. P. (2005b). The Inukshuk: A Canadian knowledge management model. *Journal of the Knowledge Management Professional Society, 2*(1), 9–16.

Girard, J. P. (2005c). Taming enterprise dementia in public sector organizations. *International Journal of Public Sector Management, 18*(6), 534–545.

Girard, J. P. (2006). Where is the knowledge we have lost in managers? *Journal of Knowledge Management, 10*(6), 22–38.

Govindarajan, V., & Trimble, C. (2006). How forgetting leads to innovation. *Chief Executive* (216), 46–49.

Gross, R. (2001). *The knowledge capital management journey at Dow.* Paper presented at the 2001 Conference on Intellectual Asset Management: How Leading Companies Realize Value from their Intellectual Assets.

Grover, V., & Davenport, T. H. (2001). General perspectives on knowledge management: Fostering a research agenda. *Journal of Management Information Systems, 18*(1), 5–21.

Hanka, R., & Fuka, K. (2000). Information overload and "just-in-time" knowledge. *The Electronic Library, 18*(4), 279–284.

Hays, C. L. (2004, November 14). What Wal-Mart knows about customers' habits. *New York Times.*

Horak, B. J. (2001). Dealing with human factors and managing change in knowledge management: A phased approach. *Topics in Health Information Management, 21*(3), 8–17.

Howe, J. (2006). The rise of crowdsourcing. *Wired, 14*(6). Retrieved January 15, 2009, from http://www.wired.com/wired/archive/14.06/crowds.html

Howe, J. (2008). *Crowdsourcing: Why the power of the crowd is driving the future of business* (1st ed.). New York: Crown Business.

InnoCenter about us. (2009). Retrieved January 15, 2009, from http://innocentive.com/about-us-open-innovation.php

Jackson, M. (2008). May we have your attention, please? *Business Week* (4089), 55–56.

Johnson, J. Our credo. Retrieved July 6, 2006, from http://www.jnj.com/our_company/our_credo/index.htm

Kaye, B., & Jacobson, B. (1999). True tales and tall tales the power of organizational storytelling. *Training & Development, 53*(3), 45–50.

Kirsh, D. (2000). A few thoughts on cognitive overload. *Intellectica (Revue de l'association pour la recherche cognitive), 30*(1), 19–51.

Kwiatkowski, R., Duncan, D. C., & Shimmin, S. (2006). What have we forgotten—and why? *Journal of Occupational & Organizational Psychology, 79*(2), 183–201.

Lacy, S., & Hempel, J. (2006, August 14). Valley Boys: Digg.com's Kevin Rose leads a new brat pack of young entrepreneurs. *Business Week*. Retrieved January 15, 2009, from http://www.businessweek.com/magazine/content/06_33/b3997001.htm

Laudon, K. C., & Laudon, J. P. (2005). *Essentials of management information systems: Managing the digital firm* (6th ed.). Upper Saddle River, NJ: Prentice Hall.

Li, C., & Bernoff, J. (2008). *Groundswell: Winning in a world transformed by social technologies.* Boston: Harvard Business Press.

Linden, A. (2001). *Information not yet at your fingertips? Here's why.* (Research Note): Gartner Research.

Linden, A., Ball, R., Arevolo, W., & Haley, K. (2002). *Gartner's survey on managing information* (Research Note): Gartner Research.

Linden, E. (1991, September 23). Lost tribes, lost knowledge. *Time Magazine, 138.*

Lotus. (2001a). ExpertLink overview. Retrieved March 14, 2002, from http://www.lotus.com/products/domworkflow.nsf/a1d792857da52f638525630f00 4e7ab8/ad9fddbda9c4bff885256aaf006054de

Lotus. (2001b). Novartis consumer health. Retrieved March 14, 2002, from http://www.lotus.com/solutions/wwwlcr.nsf/wDocs/DA3AD7D66A6F29DC8525 6A2900632B79

Lynch, K. G. (2008). *Fifteenth annual report to the prime minister on the public service of Canada.* Retrieved from http://www.pco-bcp.gc.ca/docs/information/Publications/ar-ra/15-2008/pdf/rpt_e.pdf

Mai, R., & Akerson, A. (2003). *The leader as communicator: Strategies and tactics to build loyalty, focus effort, and spark creativity.* New York: AMACOM Division American Management Association.

Maloney, S. M. (1997). *Our defended borders: A short history of the Permanent Joint Board on Defence and the Military Cooperation Committee, 1940 to present.* Ottawa: Department of National Defence.

Matsui, B. (n.d.). Action mapping, a planning tool for change. The Claremont Graduate School. Retrieved August 2, 2006, from http://www.prel.org/products/Products/ActionMapping.htm

McKee, R., & Fryer, B. (2003). Storytelling that moves people. *Harvard Business Review, 81*(6), 51–55.

Michael, H. (2002). *Teradata takes data mining beyond beer and diapers*. Dayton, OH: NCR Corporation.

Mohamed, M., Stankosky, M., & Murray, A. (2004). Applying knowledge management principles to enhance cross-functional team performance. *Journal of Knowledge Management, 8*(3), 127.

Neilson, R., & Stouffer, D. (2005). Narrating the vision scenarios in action. *The Futurist, 39*(3), 26–30.

Nonaka, I. (1991). The knowledge-creating company. *Harvard Business Review, 69*(6), 96–104.

Nonaka, I., & Konno, N. (1998). The concept of "Ba": Building a foundation for knowledge creation. *California Management Review, 40*(3), 40–54.

Nonaka, I., & Takeuchi, H. (1995). *The knowledge-creating company: How Japanese companies create the dynamics of innovation*. New York: Oxford University Press.

O'Dell, C. (2002, May 3, 2002). *Knowledge management: A new generation*. Paper presented at the APQC's 7th Knowledge Conference, Washington, DC.

O'Dell, C. (2003). *Expertise locator systems: Finding the answers* (Best-Practice Report). Houston: APQC.

O'Dell, C., Davenport, T., & Croy, N. (1997). *Using IT to support knowledge management*. Houston: APQC.

O'Dell, C., & Grayson, C. J. (1998). If only we knew what we know: Identification and transfer of internal best practices. *California Management Review, 40*(3), 154–174.

O'Dell, C., Grayson, C. J., & Essaides, N. (1998). *If only we knew what we know: The transfer of internal knowledge and best practice*. New York: Free Press.

Pan, S. L., & Scarborough, H. (1999). Knowledge management in practice: An exploratory case study. *Technology Analysis & Strategic Management, 11*(3), 359–374.

Parlby, D. (2000). *Knowledge management research report 2000*. London: KPMG Consulting.

Petch, G. (2001). The cost of lost knowledge. Retrieved September 23, 2006, from http://www.destinationkm.com/print/default.asp?ArticleID=513

Pitts, B. (2006, September 11). FDNY: The next generation. *CBS News*, Retrieved from http://www.cbsnews.com/stories/2006/09/11/eveningnews/main1999146.shtml

Plain English Campaign. Retrieved July 6, 2006, from http://www.plainenglish.co.uk

Polanyi, M. (1958). *Personal knowledge: Towards a post-critical philosophy*. Chicago: University of Chicago Press.

Rifkin, G. (1996, June/July). Buckman labs is nothing but net. *Fast Company*, 118–124.

Roberts-Witt, S. L. (2002). A "Eureka!" moment at Xerox. *PC Magazine, 21*.

Rose, K. (2007). Digg this: 09-f9-11-02-9d-74-e3-5b-d8-41-56-c5-63-56-88-c0. Retrieved January 8, 2009, from http://blog.digg.com/?p=74

Saint-Onge, H., & Wallace, D. (2003). *Leveraging communities of practice for strategic advantage*. Amsterdam; Boston: Butterworth-Heinemann.

Serson, S. (2001). *The demographics of PS executives and EX feeder groups*. Ottawa: Public Service Commission of Canada.

Snowden, D. (2002). Complex acts of knowing: Paradox and descriptive self-awareness. *Journal of Knowledge Management, 6*(2), 100–111.

Speier, C., Valacich, J. S., & Vessey, I. (1999). The influence of task interruption on individual decision making: An information overload perspective. *Decision Sciences, 30*(2), 337–360.

Stories & Storytelling. (2005). Retrieved August 2, 2006, from http://www.ivysea.com/pages/Storytelling_portal.html

Tapscott, D., & Williams, A. D. (2006). *Wikinomics: How mass collaboration changes everything*. New York: Portfolio.

Toffler, A., & Toffler, H. (1993). *War and anti-war: Survival at the dawn of the 21st century* (1st ed.). Boston: Little, Brown.

Wales, J. (2008). An appeal from Wikipedia founder. Retrieved December 24, 2008, from http://wikimediafoundation.org/wiki/Donate/Letter/en?utm_source=2008_jimmy_letter&utm_medium=sitenotice&utm_campaign=fundraiser2008#appeal

Webber, A. M. (1993). What's so new about the new economy? *Harvard Business Review, 71*(1), 24–42.

Weber, F., Wunram, M., Kemp, J., Pudlatz, M., & Bredehorst, B. (2002). *Standardisation in knowledge management—towards a common KM framework in Europe*. Paper presented at the UNICOM Seminar.

Wenger, E., McDermott, R. A., & Snyder, W. (2002). *Cultivating communities of practice: A guide to managing knowledge*. Boston: Harvard Business School Press.

White, M., & Dorman, S. M. (2000). De-densify information overload. *Education Digest, 66*(1), 27–30.

Wilson, T. D. (2001). Information overload: Implications for healthcare services. *Health Informatics Journal, 7*(2), 112–117.

Wurman, R. S. (1989). *Information anxiety*. New York: Doubleday.

Xerox. (2001a). Eureka! The story. Retrieved March 14, 2002, from http://www2.xerox.com/go/xrx/knowledgest/knowledge_section.jsp?id=19238

Xerox. (2001b). Ten domains of knowledge. Retrieved March 14, 2002, from http://www.xerox.com/go/xrx/knowledgest/knowledge_article.jsp?id=18709

Xerox. (2001c). What we know. Retrieved March 14, 2002, from http://www.xerox.com/downloads/kstreet/ks_dvp_wwknow.pdf

Index

Note: The italicized *f* following page numbers refer to figures.